Elizabeth Workman S.R.D. gained her State Registration as a dietitian after following the dietetics course at Leeds Polytechnic, already being a holder of a biological sciences degree from Leicester University. She has gained great expertise in helping people with food-related diseases and enjoys the challenge of devising appetizing and nutritious recipes from unusual ingredients, not least because her husband is a vegetarian and she caters for a growing family.

Virginia Alun Jones M.D. was research fellow to Dr Hunter at Addenbrooke's Hospital, Cambridge from 1982 until 1986. As well as contributing to this book she has presented the results of the team's work at scientific meetings in this country and Europe. She has written numerous articles for among others the *British Medical Journal*, the *Lancet*, and the *Journal of the Royal College of General Practitioners*.

John Hunter M.D. is a Consultant Physician at Addenbrooke's Hospital and a leading authority on the subject of food allergy and intolerance. He developed an interest in food in relation to diseases of the gut in response to the need of the many sufferers of irritable bowel syndrome attending his out-patients' clinic. He has contributed over 60 research papers to major medical journals including the *Lancet, Nature* and the *British Medical Journal*.

FOOD INTOLERANCE

Are the Foods You Eat
Making You Sick?
Test Yourself Using the
"Exclusion Diet"

John Hunter, M.D.;
Virginia Alun Jones, M.D.
and Elizabeth Workman, R.D.

THE BODY PRESS

To Maureen Hunter,
who contributed many of the recipes in this book

Publisher: Rick Bailey
Executive Editor: Randy Summerlin
Editor: Jacqueline Sharkey
Technical Consultant: William E. Walsh, M.D.

The Body Press, a division of HPBooks, Inc.
P.O. Box 5367
Tucson, AZ 85703
(602) 888-2150

ISBN: 0-89586-474-6

Library of Congress Catalog Card Number: 86–81046
1st Printing

Notice: The information in this book is true and complete to the
best of our knowledge. All recommendations are made without
guarantees on the part of the authors or HPBooks. The authors and
publisher disclaim all liability in connection with the use of this
information.

First published in Great Britain in 1986
by Martin Dunitz Limited,
154 Camden High Street,
London NW1 0NE

Typeset by Book Ens, Saffron Walden, England
Printed in Singapore by Toppan Printing Company (S) Pte Ltd

CONTENTS

Introduction   7

Facts about food intolerances   7
Tests for food intolerances   14
Rules for exclusion diet   17
Dietary treatment for persons with arthritis   21
Advice about restricted diets   25
Ingredients and measurements   30

The Recipes   33
Breakfasts   35
Beverages   38
Appetizers   40
Soups   47
Salads   49
Vegetables   54
Vegetarian Dishes   56
Snacks   63
Fish   68
Meat   74
Poultry   84
Stocks, Sauces & Jams   90
Bread & Pastry   96
Cakes & Cookies   100
Fruits & Puddings   112

Acknowledgments   121
Index   123

Introduction

During the last five years, medical experts have become increasingly interested in the possibility that everyday foods can cause various symptoms and illnesses. Two conditions related to food intolerance, irritable bowel syndrome and migraine headaches, affect tens of thousands of Americans. Many physicians now accept the fact that food intolerances cause problems. It is much easier for people to get medical assistance for these difficulties.

Some physicians believe too much help is available. All kinds of experts, clinics and support groups can be found. They offer advice, tests and dietary supplements. Some advocate skin tests, others hair tests or blood tests. It is hardly surprising that many people become confused.

This confusion can have unfortunate effects. In the past people suffered needlessly because they did not know that a food intolerance could make them ill. Now some people believe most illnesses are caused by food intolerance. They may spend many months and thousands of dollars searching for a dietary cure for a disease unrelated to food intolerance.

This book provides up-to-date information about the causes and effects of food intolerance. It describes specific conditions that can be affected by diet. The book also explains which food-intolerance tests may be useful and which should be avoided.

FACTS ABOUT FOOD INTOLERANCES

Most people have no food intolerances. Many people worry needlessly that what they are eating is undermining their health.

People are concerned about the effects of preservatives. However, these substances protect against food poisoning. They are not poisonous and present no problem to anyone with normal digestion.

If you are healthy and have no unpleasant symptoms, such as headaches or diarrhea, you may be quite confident that you are not suffering from any food intolerances. You should eat a normal, well-rounded, nutritious diet.

Although some people develop symptoms after eating foods such as wheat, chocolate and cheese, this does not mean that these foods are poisonous. A food intolerance is an individual reaction that causes trouble only to the person concerned – just because your friend gets an upset stomach from eating beef, that is no reason you should avoid it too.

DISTINGUISHING ALLERGIES FROM INTOLERANCES

A *food intolerance* differs from a *food allergy*. Each affects different mechanisms in the body.

Allergy   This is one type of problem that may be caused by a food or other substances, such as dust or pollen. These substances are called *allergens*. Our immune system produces antibodies that destroy bacteria or viruses entering the body. Someone with an allergy develops abnormal antibodies that react to allergens, producing allergic symptoms.

When people develop antibodies against a food, the food becomes an allergen. This is a genuine food allergy. The antibodies meet the food in question and combine with it to trigger off cells that release chemicals such as histamine. This may lead to symptoms such as wheezing or a runny nose.

In the case of allergy, the antibodies may be detected in the blood by a test called the RAST test (see page 14), so food allergy is a specific and detectable condition.

Intolerance   This is a much broader term. It includes many types of problems that may be caused by foods. Many doctors used to doubt that food caused illness because people who claimed they were allergic to a food produced negative results in the usual allergy tests. Doctors believed that these people were hypochondriacs, but in fact they were suffering a reaction to specific foods. However, the foods were not acting as allergens, so the effects did not register on traditional allergy tests.

CAUSES OF FOOD INTOLERANCES

Some foods have chemicals that can adversely affect people. One is *caffeine*, which is contained in coffee and cola drinks. People who have a caffeine intolerance may develop a rapid pulse rate, headaches, pains in their legs or indigestion after drinking coffee or cola.

Another example is *tartrazine*, the bright orange dye in some soft drinks and candies. Tartrazine can cause *urticaria*, a skin condition that can produce blotches and swelling of the lips or the mouth. It can also cause *eczema*, a skin disease whose symptoms include itching, blistering and scaling. Tartrazine may also produce behavior changes in young children. However, tartrazine produces no adverse effects in the vast majority of the population.

Enzyme deficiencies can also cause problems. *Enzymes* are the chemicals that help digestion. Some people don't have one or more enzymes. For example, in some people, the enzyme that digests, *lactose*, the sugar that is in milk, disappears from the intestine as they grow into adulthood. People who lack this enzyme may develop diarrhea and stomach pains after drinking milk.

People taking antibiotics may also develop intolerances. We recently completed an extensive study of the causes of irritable bowel syndrome, whose symptoms include diarrhea and abdominal pain resulting from food intolerance. We noticed that women who had recently had a hysterectomy frequently suffered from this problem. Antibiotics are often prescribed after this operation to treat infection, and they are very effective. However, we were able to show that women who received antibiotics were more likely to develop irritable bowel syndrome. We found that the bacteria in their intestines were different from those of women who had not developed this problem.

We believe that antibiotics may lead to food intolerances in some patients. The antibiotics apparently kill some types of bacteria in the large intestine and allow other types to flourish. These bacteria may react differently during digestion and produce unpleasant chemicals that cause various symptoms. Of course, this is not a reason for refusing to take antibiotics if you really need them. However, it is a very strong argument for taking antibiotics only when necessary.

EFFECTS OF FOOD INTOLERANCE

Many medical experts believe that food intolerance can cause or contribute to various illnesses. These illnesses include:

Irritable Bowel Syndrome   This is sometimes called *spastic colon*. The symptoms include abdominal pain and distention, diarrhea and changes in bowel habits. People often develop symptoms after gastroenteritis or long courses of antibiotics. This condition is more common among women than men.

Migraine Headache   This is a severe headache that usually affects one side of the head. Associated symptoms are nausea and vomiting.

Asthma   This involves wheezing and shortness of breath. At night, these symptoms may be accompanied by coughing.

Rhinitis   This is the medical term for a persistently runny or stuffed-up nose. The symptoms are similar to those of a common cold, but do not disappear in a week or two. They are chronic.

Gluten Sensitive Enteropathy   This is a condition in which gluten, a protein found in wheat, rye and barley, damages the lining of the small intestine so food is not properly absorbed. It can lead to diarrhea, bone disease, stunted growth, weight loss and possibly anemia.

CONDITIONS CAUSED BY FOOD INTOLERANCES

- Irritable bowel syndrome
- Migraine headache
- Asthma
- Rhinitis
- Gluten sensitive enteropathy
- Eczema

- Urticaria
- Cow's milk sensitive enteropathy
- Crohn's disease
- Some types of arthritis
- Hyperactivity in children

Eczema   This illness is characterized by an itching red rash, often on the insides of elbows and knees, which may scale and crust.

Urticaria   This involves large, red, itchy blotches that can appear anywhere on the body. Urticaria can also cause the lips and mouth to swell.

Cow's Milk Sensitive Enteropathy   This usually affects babies who are bottle-fed cow's milk before the age of 4 months. Symptoms are severe stomach pain, diarrhea, eczema, vomiting and a runny nose.
    Doctors have thought for some time that food intolerance could cause these illnesses. Recent evidence indicates that food intolerance might contribute to other conditions. These include Crohn's disease, some types of arthritis and hyperactivity in children.

Crohn's Disease   This is an inflammation of the gut, which most often involves the *ileum*, the lower part of the small intestine. The number of people with this disease has increased enormously in the last 30 years. An estimated 8 people in every 100,000 now have Crohn's disease. It usually affects children and young adults. More women have it than men. Symptoms include diarrhea, abdominal pain, weight loss and anemia. The bowel may become narrowed, leading to obstruction. Until recently surgery to remove the diseased part of the bowel has been the only successful treatment. Drugs such as steroids might temporarily alleviate the disease, but they often have unpleasant side effects.
    Recently, however, we found some evidence that Crohn's disease is related to diet. We made the discovery about diet and Crohn's disease by accident. A young woman who came to our clinic in Cambridge, England, was suffering from symptoms that we believed were caused by irritable bowel syndrome. We ran tests and put her on the exclusion diet listed on page 19 while awaiting the results. When the tests indicated she had Crohn's disease, we called her back to the clinic to start a course of steroids. When she came in, it was obvious her condition had improved dramatically. Her symptoms had been aggravated by wheat. After she stopped eating foods containing wheat, her

symptoms disappeared. She has remained well for over six years.

We have now successfully treated more than 100 people by changing their diet. Not everyone with Crohn's disease is intolerant to wheat. Some patients are intolerant to other cereals, dairy products or several foods.

Many victims of Crohn's disease who come to our clinic are undernourished. We first build them up with a special diet called an elemental diet. It comprises food that has been broken down to its constituent chemicals, such as amino acids, fatty acids and sugars, plus minerals and vitamins. After one or two weeks on this diet, many people find that their symptoms disappear. We then begin tests to ascertain which foods are aggravating the problem.

We have successfully treated 80 percent of Crohn's disease patients by changing their diets. However, 20 percent need other types of treatment. Diet will not cure an abscess or severe narrowing of the bowel. Surgery is required for these conditions. Anyone suffering from Crohn's disease should consult a physician before starting any diet. This is especially important if a person has become undernourished. A physician will be able to prescribe a diet to help the patient regain strength. He or she may also need vitamin and mineral supplements. After the situation has improved, the patient will have to consult a physician and a dietitian to work out the proper diet. We do not recommend people with Crohn's disease try to treat themselves by following an exclusion diet without medical support. Nevertheless, anyone with Crohn's disease who is being treated by dietary measures will find the information and recipes in this book extremely useful.

Arthritis Many people are confused about the meaning of the word *arthritis*. It means inflammation of the joints. There are numerous forms of arthritis. No diet can alleviate them all. Diet can sometimes help because arthritis affects the immune system.

Osteoarthritis is probably the most common form of the disease, especially among women. Many experts believe osteoarthritis is caused by wear and tear on the joints, especially the hips and knees. This type of arthritis usually will not be alleviated by diet. The one exception involves obese patients, who sometimes feel better after losing weight.

Gout is a type of arthritis caused by deposits of uric acid crystals in the joints. The uric acid comes from the breakdown of chemicals known as *purines*. Many physicians now treat gout with drugs that block the formation of uric acid or increase its excretion in the urine. However, some still recommend a diet that excludes foods rich in purines. Such foods include organ meats such as liver and kidneys, peas, beans, sardines, anchovies and herrings.

Rheumatoid arthritis   This disease is characterized by pain and tenderness in active joints in the hands, wrists, elbows, shoulders, ankles and feet. It is three times more common in women than men.

Attempts to treat rheumatoid arthritis through diet have caused considerable controversy. Several diets have been promoted by doctors and herbalists, but none has proved entirely successful.

Numerous physicians have reported that a few rheumatoid arthritis patients have found that their problems were caused by foods. However, many other patients experience short-term improvement because of the *placebo effect* – they believe a treatment will help them, so it does.

We have adapted an exclusion diet specifically for arthritis patients. Seven out of 12 patients have improved on this diet. Details of the diet are provided on page 22.

Hyperactivity   Many people call any child who is energetic and noisy "hyperactive". However, most of these children are over-active, not hyperactive. *Overactivity*, which results from excessive energy, is very different from *hyperactivity*, a condition requiring treatment.

Most hyperactive children are boys ages 1 to 7. Their condition is characterized by intense physical activity, poor concentration, behavioral problems and temper tantrums. Other symptoms include poor eating and sleeping habits, abnormal thirst, learning disabilities, headaches, asthma, hay fever, sputum and nasal discharge.

The most famous findings about diet and hyperactivity were made by Dr. Ben Feingold, a U.S. researcher. He linked hyperactivity to artificial food colors and flavors, aspirin, and natural salicylates in some fruits and vegetables. Hyperactivity has also been linked to other factors, including dust and chemicals in aerosols, disinfectants and perfume. Dr. Feingold designed a diet for hyperactive children that was very effective in some cases.

Many pediatricians working with hyperactive children have dismissed the Feingold diet. Evidence of its effectiveness is mixed. However, researchers at the Hospital for Sick Children in London reported considerable success using dietary treatment with hyperactive children. They reported that of 76 children treated, 21 recovered, 41 improved and 14 showed no improvement. These children were on a much stricter diet than Dr. Feingold's. The diet eliminated not only additives, but foods such as cow's milk, chocolate, wheat, oranges, cheese and eggs. However, many children were allowed to have sugar. Researchers found that sugar had little effect on most of the children.

A hyperactive child might improve by following the exclusion diet on page 17. This diet eliminates all food that may be contributing to the child's condition. By reintroducing the foods gradually, as instructed, a physician may find which foods are actually involved.

It is crucial that parents consult a physician before putting a child on an exclusion diet. The final diet must always be checked by a trained dietitian who will work under the supervision of the physician. This is especially important because growing children have special nutritional needs. Vitamin and mineral supplements may be required. For example, a child may have to take calcium tablets if an acceptable milk substitute cannot be found.

TESTS FOR FOOD INTOLERANCE

Because foods may cause symptoms in different ways, a person may have to undergo several tests to determine whether he or she has a food intolerance. Many tests are available, but not all of them are effective for every type of case. It is important to be familiar with the basic types of tests and their limitations. They include the following:

Skin Tests   These were developed by allergists during the early 20th century. These tests involve injecting an extract of a suspected food into the skin. This is done by putting a small quantity on the skin and pricking through, or by injecting a small amount beneath the skin. If the test is positive, the site of the injection swells, and the area around it becomes inflamed. Because only one skin prick is necessary for each food, many foods can be tested during one office visit.

This test can be very useful when someone has a food allergy. However, it will not help a physician diagnose other conditions. A person lacking the enzyme that breaks down milk sugar will have no reaction to a skin test. Many people with food-related conditions such as migraine, diarrhea and hyperactivity will have negative skin tests.

Because most people don't know whether they have a food allergy or a food intolerance, skin tests are probably not the best tests to start with. Another drawback is that these tests are expensive.

Tongue Test   This is a modification of the skin test. Food is placed under the tongue to see whether it produces a reaction. This test has not proved reliable.

Radioallergosorbent Test (RAST)   This is a more sophisticated form of skin test, but is more limited because it measures only some immediate reactions to food. It may not pick up delayed reactions. Blood from people with a food allergy contains antibodies to the foods concerned. These can be detected in the laboratory. However, the RAST test, like the skin test, is negative in people who have a food intolerance rather than a food allergy.

Cytotoxic Test   This test involves mixing a blood sample from the patient with food extracts. Technicians then observe changes in the blood cells under a microscope. Because only a small quantity of blood is required, a series of tests may be done with one sample.

However, researchers have not yet confirmed whether the blood cells of people with food intolerances react with food chemicals. Independent scientific studies indicate that this test is unreliable. We have also found it ineffective. Many people come to our clinic claiming that their blood cells reacted to food samples in a cytotoxic test and that, therefore, they cannot eat specific foods. However, we have found that when they eat those foods, they suffer no adverse reactions. We decided to do a *blind test* on one woman who had been told she had a wheat intolerance. In a blind test, the participant is not told what he or she is taking. We gave this woman wheat extract and she had no reaction.

Hair Tests Many laboratories say they can diagnose food intolerances by analyzing the minerals in a specimen of hair. Minerals such as mercury, cadmium and arsenic are deposited in hair as it grows. Some researchers believe that mineral deficiencies are the reason why some people have adverse reactions to specific foods.

The amount of minerals in a person's hair sometimes reflects the amount in his or her body at the time the hair began to grow. However, if a person has long hair, their hair may have been growing for months.

The link between mineral deficiencies and food intolerances has not been proven. If you have a hair analysis done, you must still confirm that the suspected foods are actually causing the problems. We believe hair tests are unreliable and do not recommend them. Their principal value is to detect the presence of arsenic in murder victims!

Blood Analysis Numerous minerals can be detected in the blood. Laboratories offering to analyze blood samples use the same rationale as laboratories offering to analyze hair. They claim mineral deficiencies cause adverse reactions to food. However, medical experts do not yet fully understand the significance of mineral levels in the blood. For example, they know zinc is very important in the formation of various enzymes, but they don't know how much zinc is needed or exactly how it works. Many people with low levels of zinc in their blood do not appear to benefit when extra zinc is added to their diet.

The role of many other minerals is even more of a mystery. Because of this, we do not think mineral analysis can accurately detect food intolerance.

Dietary Tests These are the only effective tests for diagnosing food intolerance. Many foods affect people differently. The only accurate way to see whether a food is producing an adverse reaction is to have a person eat that food and see what happens. We have had considerable success diagnosing patients at our clinic with this technique. We then treat people by modifying their diet. Our success rate is 70 percent.

If you believe you may have a food intolerance, ask your physician if you could start on our exclusion diet. If this is successful and your condition improves, you can reintroduce foods into your diet one at a time. This should enable you and your physician to discover which foods have been causing your problems.

The exclusion diet is outlined on the following pages. In addition to helping you detect food intolerances, this diet will also provide vitamins, minerals and other nutrients that you need for good health. Arthritis sufferers who wish to try this type of diet should follow the special instructions on page 22.

RULES FOR EXCLUSION DIET

Anyone on the exclusion diet should observe the following rules:

1. For the first two weeks, eat *only* the foods allowed. These foods are listed on page 19. It is essential to do this for the entire two-week period. If you take a day off, you will have to start again from the beginning.

2. If you believe any of the allowed foods are causing adverse reactions, also exclude these foods the first two weeks.

3. During the second week on the exclusion diet eat a variety of allowed foods. Keep a diary listing what foods you eat, what symptoms you have and when the symptoms occur. You should experience steady improvement during the second week. Any setbacks during this time will probably have been caused by foods eaten during the previous 24 hours.

4. If your symptoms haven't improved after two weeks, it is unlikely that food intolerance is the cause of your problem. Resume your normal eating patterns and ask your doctor about other treatment.

5. If your symptoms have improved after 14 days, you can begin the reintroduction phase of the treatment program. This will enable you and your physician and dietitian to ascertain which foods caused your problems.

RULES FOR REINTRODUCING FOODS

1. You must reintroduce foods into your diet in the order listed in the chart on page 20.

2. Continue keeping your diary. List the foods eaten, any symptoms you have and the times such symptoms occur. This is *very* important.

3. How many foods you can reintroduce at one time depends on which condition you have. If you have suffered from migraine, irritable bowel syndrome, asthma, rhinitis or hyperactivity, you should introduce one food every two days. If you have suffered from eczema or urticaria, you should introduce one food a week. If you suffer from Crohn's disease, you should introduce one food a day starting with the foods allowed on the exclusion diet, and gradually reducing the amount of elemental diet taken each day.

4. Symptoms develop over different periods of time. Don't expect to experience a symptom immediately after you have eaten a specific food. Sometimes symptoms appear so slowly that they are barely noticeable. Sometimes they appear only after you

have been eating a food for several days. If you begin experiencing symptoms, look in your diary to see when you last felt really well. This will help you and your physician track down the food that has caused the problem.

5. Eat plenty of each food that you test. If you have experienced no symptoms after the last test day, you may assume that these foods are safe to eat in normal quantities.

6. If a food has more than one ingredient, try to test each ingredient before testing the food.

7. If you have an adverse reaction to a food, flush out your system by drinking plenty of water. Some people find that adding a little baking soda helps.

8. At the end of the reintroduction phase of the treatment program, retest any food you think might have affected you. This will enable you and your doctor to make more exact judgments about which foods are causing problems.

9. After identifying these foods, ask your doctor to arrange a consultation with a dietitian to ensure that the diet you are planning to follow is nutritionally adequate.

RULES FOR FOLLOW-UP DIET

After ascertaining which foods affect you adversely, you need to exclude only these foods from your diet. If you have problems with only one or two foods, this should not be too difficult. As you will probably have discovered during the exclusion diet, delicious substitutes are available for most foods. You just need to experiment and give yourself a chance to become accustomed to new flavors and textures. The recipes and suggestions in this book will help you. If you find you are intolerant to many foods, you will have to discuss the situation with your doctor and dietitian to ensure that a diet to control your symptoms will be nutritionally adequate.

If you have gluten sensitive enteropathy, you must always adhere to a gluten-free diet to avoid damaging your small intestine.

INTOLERANCES CAN CHANGE

Remember that food intolerances can come and go. Some people discover that after excluding a food for several months they lose their intolerance. Try reintroducing foods you have been avoiding every six months to see whether they still cause adverse reactions.

Unfortunately, it is also possible to develop new intolerances. We believe that surgical procedures, courses of antibiotics, viral

FOODS FOR THE ADDENBROOKE'S EXCLUSION DIET

Lists of foods containing prohibited ingredients are on pages 27–9

TYPE OF FOOD	NOT ALLOWED	ALLOWED
Meat	Preserved meats, bacon, sausages	All other meats
Fish	Smoked fish, shellfish	White fish
Vegetables	Potatoes, onions, corn	All other vegetables, including legumes such as beans, lentils, peas; rutabaga, parsnips; salads
Fruit	Citrus fruits, such as oranges, grapefruit	All other fruit, including apples, bananas, pears*
Cereals	Wheat, oats, barley, rye, corn	Rice, ground rice, rice flakes, rice flour, sago, Rice Krispies, tapioca, millet, buck-wheat, rice cakes
Cooking oils	Corn oil, vegetable oil	Sunflower oil, soy oil, olive oil, safflower oil
Dairy products	Cow's milk, butter, most margarines, cow's milk yogurt and cheese, eggs	Goat's milk†, soy milk, sheep's milk, kosher margarine, goat's and sheep's milk yogurt and cheese, soy cheese
Beverages	Coffee and tea, instant and decaffeinated; soft drinks, orange juice, grapefruit juice, alcohol, tap water (except for cooking)	Some herbal teas, fresh fruit juices, such as apple, pineapple, tomato juice, mineral, distilled or deionized water
Miscellaneous	Chocolate, yeast, preservatives, nuts	Carob, sea salt, herbs, spices, and honey and sugar in moderation

* Some fruits, especially overripe ones, contain small amounts of yeast, but the quantities rarely cause any problems.

† A few people at our clinic have reported that goat's milk has caused adverse reactions. We recommend soy milk instead of goat's milk. Some people have no problem with goat's milk. However, we advise anyone with a milk intolerance to be especially careful.

REINTRODUCTION OF FOODS

Order of reintroduction:

1. Tap water
2. Potatoes
3. Cow's milk
4. Yeast – take 3 brewer's yeast tablets or 2 teaspoons baker's yeast in water
5. Tea
6. Rye – test rye crackers and, if yeast was negative, rye bread
7. Butter
8. Onions
9. Eggs
10. Oats – test rolled oats
11. Coffee – test coffee beans and instant coffee separately
12. Chocolate – test plain chocolate
13. Barley – test pearl barley, added to soups and stews
14. Citrus fruits
15. Corn – test cornstarch or corn on the cob
16. Cow's cheese
17. White wine
18. Shellfish
19. Cow's yogurt – test natural yogurt, not flavored
20. Vinegar
21. Wheat – test as whole-wheat bread, or if yeast is a problem, test wheat flakes. Wheat produces its effects slowly, so test for twice as long as other foods.
22. Nuts
23. Preservatives – fruit, soft drinks, canned foods, monosodium glutamate, saccharin, aspartame

---

infections and gastroenteritis can contribute to the development of food intolerances. If you develop symptoms, you may have to go through the testing process again to discover what is causing the problems.

DIETARY TREATMENT FOR PERSONS WITH ARTHRITIS

As mentioned previously, claims have been made that various diets relieve symptoms of rheumatoid arthritis. Such claims are often made about diets eaten in countries where arthritis is rare. Unfortunately, most of these claims are not backed up by rigorous, scientific testing. Diets that have been touted as beneficial for arthritis sufferers include:

Dr. Dong's Diet This was devised in the 1940s and is based on the diet of people in China, where arthritis is relatively rare. It is rich in fish and excludes red meat, fruits, egg yolk, dairy products, additives, spices and chocolate. Although many people have claimed that this diet has helped them, a controlled study failed to reveal any differences between those who followed the Dong program and those who ate an ordinary diet.

Although this diet is nutritionally adequate, we believe it excludes so many foods that people will be unwilling to follow it indefinitely. It lacks the flexibility of the exclusion diet. There is no reason to avoid a food unless you are sure that eating it causes problems.

The Eskimo Diet Because Eskimos eat a great deal of fish and seldom suffer from arthritis, some people have suggested that enriching the diet with the polyunsaturated fatty acids found in fish might alleviate arthritis symptoms. However, a recent study reported in *The Lancet* showed that the benefits of this diet were limited. The treatment group had less morning stiffness and fewer tender joints after 12 weeks on this diet, but when they resumed their normal eating habits, they appeared to deteriorate more quickly than the other group, which ate a typical American diet.

The Acid-Reducing Diet This is based on the idea that the acids produced in the body during digestion contribute to arthritis. It is true that doctors recommend that patients with gout avoid foods that contribute to formation of uric acid crystals. Otherwise, no other proof of the acid-reducing theory exists. The acid-reducing diet differs from Dr. Dong's in that it encourages consumption of dairy products and excludes fish, tea and coffee. Apart from this, the diets are very similar and equally lacking in scientific support.

THE EXCLUSION DIET FOR ARTHRITIS

Arthritis cannot be totally controlled by diet. However, many people claim that diet has alleviated their symptoms. Therefore, we have prepared a diet for arthritis sufferers that is nutritionally adequate and will provide a starting point for people who wish to see whether specific foods are aggravating their symptoms.

We are confident that people with arthritis who wish to see whether dietary changes can alleviate their symptoms will suffer no adverse reactions by adhering to the diet outlined below for three weeks. However, we believe anyone who wishes to try this diet should check first with their physician. After adhering to this diet for 21 days, you begin reintroducing and testing foods. You should do so in the order listed on page 24. Each food should be tested for four days. Eat plenty of each food being tested. If your symptoms do not return after this time, you can assume the food is safe in normal quantities.

It is very important for anyone following this diet to continue taking any prescribed medication until it is quite clear that the diet has relieved arthritis symptoms. Be sure to check with your physician before stopping medication. If you do stop medication too soon, you may suffer considerable pain.

FOODS FOR THE ADDENBROOKE'S EXCLUSION DIET FOR ARTHRITIS

Foods eaten should be fresh or frozen. Canned and packaged foods should be avoided if they contain additives.

TYPE OF FOOD	NOT ALLOWED	ALLOWED
Meat	Red meat, such as beef, pork, lamb; preserved meat, sausages	Chicken, rabbit, turkey
Fish	Smoked fish, shellfish	White fish
Vegetables	Onions, tomatoes	All other vegetables, including legumes such as beans, lentils, peas; potatoes, salads
Fruit	Citrus fruit, such as oranges, grapefruit	All other fruits, including apples, bananas, pears*

TYPE OF FOOD	NOT ALLOWED	ALLOWED
Cereals	Wheat, rye, oats, barley, corn, rice, ground rice	Tapioca, sago, millet, buckwheat
Cooking oils	Corn oil, vegetable oil	Sunflower oil, soy oil, olive oil, safflower oil
Dairy products	Cow's milk, butter, most margarines, cow's milk yogurt, and cheese, eggs	Soy milk, kosher margarine, goat's milk products, including yogurt and cheese;† sheep's milk products
Beverages	Coffee and tea, instant and decaffeinated; soft drinks, orange juice, grapefruit juice, tomato juice, alcohol, tap water (except for cooking)	Some herbal teas, fresh fruit juices, including apple and pineapple; mineral, distilled or deionized water
Miscellaneous	Sugar, chocolate, yeast, yeast extract, nuts, flavored toothpaste, preservatives	Salt, pepper, herbs, spices, in moderation

* Some fruits, especially overripe ones, contain small amounts of yeast, but the quantities rarely cause problems.

† A few people at our clinic have reported that goat's milk has caused adverse reactions. We recommend soy milk instead of goat's milk. However, we advise anyone with a milk intolerance to be especially careful.

REINTRODUCTION OF FOODS FOR ARTHRITIS

Order of reintroduction:

1. Milk
2. Tea
3. Tap water
4. Lamb
5. Rice
6. Butter
7. Onions
8. Beef
9. Eggs
10. Yeast – take 3 brewer's yeast tablets or 2 teaspoons baker's yeast in water
11. Rye – test rye crackers and, if yeast was negative, test rye bread
12. Coffee – test coffee beans and instant coffee separately
13. Pork
14. Wheat – test whole-wheat bread, or, if yeast is a problem, test wheat flakes. Wheat produces its effects slowly, so test for twice as long as other foods
15. Chocolate – test plain chocolate
16. Citrus fruit
17. Tomatoes
18. Cheese
19. Corn – test cornstarch or corn on the cob
20. White wine
21. Shellfish
22. Sugar
23. Oats – test rolled oats
24. Yogurt
25. Nuts
26. Preservatives – soft drinks, canned foods, sausages, smoked fish, saccharin, aspartame

ADVICE ABOUT RESTRICTED DIETS

This section of the book will help you shop for the proper foods. Be sure to follow these tips:

ALWAYS CHECK THE LABEL

The exclusion diet charts tell you which foods not to eat. However, some of these foods are contained in manufactured products. It is extremely important to check the ingredients of every food product to see whether they contain forbidden items.

The chart on page 27–9 provides some guidelines about the products most likely to contain prohibited items. If you are in doubt about any ingredient, do not eat that food.

TYPES OF ACCEPTABLE FOODS

At first it may seem that the exclusion diet will be almost impossible to follow, because so many familiar foods are not allowed. The recipes in this book will show you how to prepare interesting and nutritious meals while you are trying to diagnose your food intolerances.

Many of the recipes contain unusual ingredients. You may think they will be difficult to find. However, many foods used in the recipes are available in your supermarket. The availability of foods will vary from one part of the country to another and at different times of the year.

Canned Foods　A few people report that some foods produce no adverse reactions when fresh or frozen, but can cause problems in canned form. For this reason, we have been reluctant to use canned food in our recipes. However, officials of the Food Preservation Institute, located in England, say they have no explanation for this. They point out that laws concerning food preparation, preservation, labeling and sale are quite strict in England and the United States. Therefore, we have extended the list of foods available from the supermarkets and drugstores to encourage you to test canned foods. They can make it easier for you to adhere to your diet.

COOKING UTENSILS AND FOOD CONTAINERS

No evidence exists that any cooking utensils or food containers affect people with food intolerances. Some studies indicate that aluminum is related to *Alzheimer's disease*. Some experts believe aluminum is dangerous because the metal tends to come off with use. However, this is an environmental concern rather than a factor relating to food intolerance. Our experience indicates that it is safe to use any cooking utensils and containers.

FOODS TO AVOID OR BE WARY OF ON A RESTRICTED DIET

The following foods are likely to contain forbidden ingredients. Avoid the foods in column 1. Always check the labels of foods in column 2.

Ingredient	*Foods containing the ingredient*	*Foods likely to contain the ingredient*
Wheat*	Bread: white, whole-wheat, whole-grain Cakes and cookies	Beverages: cocoa, chocolate, 'bedtime' drinks Rye bread, wafers
	Fish: cooked in batter, bread crumbs, batter or sauce Flours & cereals: ordinary wheat flours, bran, wheat germ, semolina, pasta, noodles	Cheese: spread, processed Fish: canned, paste Fruit: pie fillings Meat: canned, packaged, lunch-meats, pâté, sausages, paste
	Meat: pies, sausage rolls Pastry Desserts: pudding mixes	Desserts: ice cream, mousses, custard powder
	Soups: canned and packaged	Vegetables: canned in sauce, instant mashed potatoes
	Miscellaneous: stuffings, packaged seasonings, pepper compounds	Miscellaneous: spreads (sweet and savory), curry powder, gravy powder, bouillon cubes, baking powder, bottled sauces

---

* Products with any of the following listed on the label probably contain wheat: wheat starch, edible starch, cereal filler, cereal binder, cereal protein.

Ingredient	Foods containing the ingredient	Foods likely to contain the ingredient
Yeast	Any bread except soda bread Any products containing bread Buns made with yeast Dairy products: cheese, buttermilk, sour cream, yogurt, synthetic creams Fermented beverages: wine, beer Fruit juices: canned, bottled, in cartons Grapes, currants, plums, golden raisins, dates and prunes, overripe fruit Malted milk drinks Meat products containing bread: sausages, meat loaf, hamburgers Vinegar and pickled foods Bottled sauces Yeast extract	Vitamin products: most B vitamin products contain yeast
Corn†	Bleached white flour Cornflakes Cornstarch Pudding mixes Brown gravy mixes Margarine, vegetable oil and salad dressings containing corn oil Candies sweetened with corn syrup	Baking: cake and cookie mixes, cakes, cookies, baking powder Bottled sauces Cakes and cookies Ice creams Instant puddings Jams, jellies and spreads Tortillas

---

† Products with any of the following listed on the label probably contain corn: cornstarch, corn oil, corn syrup, cornmeal, edible starch, food starch, corn oil, glucose syrup, vegetable oil, dextrose.

Ingredient	Foods containing the ingredient	Foods likely to contain the ingredient
Cow's milk and cow's milk products ●	Malted milk drinks Custard Milk chocolate	Biscuits Bread, bread mixes Breakfast cereals Baking: cake and cookie mixes, cakes, cookies Gravy mixes Puddings, pudding mixes Ice cream T.V. dinners and other ready-to-eat meals Sauces Soups Sausages Candies: fudge, toffee Vegetables canned in sauce
Eggs (yolk, white or lecithin)	Cakes Pastry Batter Egg noodles, pasta Mayonnaise	Cookies Malted milk drinks Puddings, pudding mixes Soups

● Products with any of the following listed on the label contain cow's milk: milk, butter, margarine, cream cheese, yogurt, skim milk powder, non-fat milk solids, caseinates, whey, lactalbumin, lactose.

INGREDIENTS AND MEASUREMENTS

In addition to the basic ingredients for cooking on an exclusion diet we have found the following. These should be available in supermarkets or health food stores.

Carob Sweets   Carob-coated sweets are a good substitute for chocolate bars. There are many types available, including carob-coated rice cakes and fruit bars. However, the carob coating contains milk. Do not buy these if you are following the exclusion or milk-free diets.

Egg Substitutes   We have not used these in the recipes in this book because they are not suitable for the exclusion diet. However, people following an egg-free diet alone may find them useful.

Garam Masala   This is a mixed spice frequently used in Indian cooking. It is not available everywhere in the United States, but can be made in a coffee grinder.

4 cardamom pods
1 (3-inch) piece cinnamon stick
1 chili pepper
½ teaspoon whole cloves
1 teaspoon ground coriander
1 teaspoon ground cumin
2 bay leaves

Preheat broiler. Place all ingredients on broiler pan. Broil 2 minutes. Allow to cool. Place in coffee grinder; grind to a powder. Store in airtight container.

Gluten-Free Products   These include gluten-free breads, cookies and pastas. Such items can be made from *wheat-free starch*, which is wheat with the gluten removed, or from different flours, such as potato, rice or soy flour. Always check the ingredients to make sure they are suitable for you. We would not recommend that you use anything containing wheat starch if you are on a wheat-free diet.

Ground Rice   This is difficult to find in the United States, but you can make it by putting regular rice in a blender or food processor fitted with a steel blade and processing at medium speed for about 19 seconds.

Milk-Free Margarines These are made from vegetable oils and contain no animal fats. Some contain wheat-germ oil and should not be used if you are on the exclusion or wheat-free diet.

Miso This is a wheat-free flavoring made from rice.

Soy Products There are many soy desserts, such as rice puddings, custards and soy ice cream. Always read the ingredients to be sure the product is safe for you. You can make your own soy milk from soy flour.

Tofu This is soy curd. It is very versatile and can be used in many dishes. You will find a number of recipes using tofu in this book.

Wheat-Free Tamari This is also made from soybeans and is a useful flavoring in some dishes. It can be used on the exclusion diet.

COOKING GRAINS

Brown Rice Wash and drain rice. Put rice into twice its volume of water. Bring the water to a boil, add rice and ½ to 1 teaspoon salt, depending on quantity being cooked. Reduce heat, cover and simmer for about 40 minutes until tender and water is absorbed. Do not stir rice while it is cooking; this breaks up the grains. Fluff with a fork when ready.

Buckwheat This grain can be bought either roasted or unroasted. The roasted is stronger in flavor. The type you choose depends on your preference. Put buckwheat into twice its volume of cold salted water; bring to a boil. Reduce heat, cover and simmer until all the moisture has been absorbed and buckwheat is soft (about 15 minutes). Unroasted buckwheat takes slightly longer to cook than roasted. Do not stir while cooking.

Millet Cook as for buckwheat. In some savory dishes, millet can be dry roasted in the pan first to enhance the flavor.

The Recipes

Recipes do not include artificial coloring, flavoring, preservatives, gluten (wheat, rye or barley), other wheat, corn, oats or cow's milk. If you want to exclude one or more of these from your diet, you may use any recipe. If you are following the first stage of the exclusion diet or are excluding eggs, you should select only those appropriately marked. If other foods are to be excluded, you will need to examine the list of ingredients in each recipe to see whether the recipe is suitable.

When the recipe calls for a milk substitute, use any suitable alternative, such as goat's, sheep's or soy milk.

SYMBOLS

The symbols for special diets are:

★ Exclusion

W Wheat-free

M Milk-free

E Egg-free

A Arthritis

Breakfasts

Muesli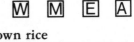

1½ cups millet flakes
1 scant cup buckwheat

½ cup brown rice
⅔ cup packed, mixed dried fruit

Cook millet, buckwheat and rice according to instructions (see page 31). Allow to cool. Mix with chopped dried fruit. Serve with milk substitute. Makes 6 servings.

Granola W M E

2 cups millet flakes
1 cup hazelnuts, chopped
6 tablespoons honey
2 tablespoons molasses
1 tablespoon soybean oil

⅔ cup packed mixed chopped
  dried fruit (including
  apricots, dates, raisins)

Preheat oven to 350F (175C).
  Place millet flakes, nuts, honey, molasses and oil in a medium bowl. Mix well. Spread mixture thinly over 2 baking sheets. Bake in preheated oven 30 minutes, turning occasionally so that millet is evenly and lightly browned. Allow granola to cool. Mix in dried fruit. Store in a sealed jar for up to 1 month. Makes 4 cups.

Tip

Serve as a breakfast cereal with milk or on top of yogurt or fruit as a dessert.

Raspberry & Millet Crunch

4 tablespoons kosher margarine
1 cup millet flakes

⅓ cup brown sugar, packed
2⅓ cups raspberries

Melt the margarine in a small skillet; add millet and cook over medium heat until golden brown. Allow to cool, then stir in sugar.

———▶

Divide ½ the raspberries between individual glass dishes and cover with ½ millet mixture; repeat with remaining millet mixture and raspberries. Chill in the refrigerator. Makes 4 servings.

Tip

Good served with goat's milk or ewe's milk yogurt.

Buckwheat Pancakes

8 tablespoons buckwheat flour	1 egg
8 tablespoons rice flour	1¼ cups milk substitute
Pinch of salt	⅔ tablespoon oil

In a medium bowl, sift together flours and salt. Add egg and milk substitute; beat well. Let stand 30 minutes.

Place about ⅔ tablespoon oil in a medium skillet. Heat until oil just begins to smoke. Quickly pour in enough batter to coat base of skillet thinly; tilt pan to make sure batter coats skillet evenly. Let pancake set and brown underneath. Turn pancake over with a spatula and cook the other side. Makes 4 pancakes.

Date & Apple Filled Pancakes

2 tablespoons kosher margarine	½ teaspoon pumpkin-pie spice
2⅔ cups Golden Delicious apples, peeled, cored and sliced	½ cup dates, chopped
	4 Buckwheat Pancakes (see above)
4 tablespoons dark brown sugar	2 tablespoons honey

Preheat oven to 350F (175C).

Melt margarine in medium saucepan. Add apples, sugar, pumpkin-pie spice and dates. Cook over low heat 10 to 15 minutes, stirring frequently, until apples are soft.

Lay pancakes on a flat surface. Spoon apple mixture onto one side of each pancake. Roll up loosely and arrange in a baking tray. Warm honey; spoon it over pancakes to glaze. Bake in preheated oven until heated through, about 15 minutes. Makes 4 servings.

Apricot Filled Pancakes

1½ cups dried apricots	4 Buckwheat Pancakes (see above)
⅓ cup light brown sugar	
¾ cup water	2 tablespoons honey

Preheat oven to 350F (175C).

Soak apricots in a bowl of cold water several hours. Drain. Place apricots in a medium saucepan with brown sugar and water. Cover; bring to a boil. Simmer until soft, 20 to 30 minutes.

Lay pancakes on a flat surface and spoon apricots onto one side of each pancake. Roll up loosely; arrange in a baking dish. Warm honey; spoon over pancakes to glaze. Bake in preheated oven until heated through, about 15 minutes. Makes 4 servings.

Mixed Dried Fruit   ★ W M E

2½ cups unsweetened apple juice
2 tablespons sugar
1 (2-inch) cinnamon stick

1 cup dried apricots
⅔ cup dried prunes
¾ cup dried figs
¾ cup dried apples, chopped

Place apple juice in a medium saucepan over low heat. Add sugar and stir until it has dissolved. Add cinnamon. Place dried fruit in a medium bowl and pour syrup over. Cover; leave to soak 24 hours. Refrigerate until chilled. Makes 6 servings.

Tip

If soaked fruit is not tender, place in a medium saucepan over medium heat and simmer for several minutes.

Breakfast Fruit Soup   W M E

3 tablespoons tapioca
2 tablespoons sugar
2½ cups water
¾ cup unsweetened orange juice

1 banana, sliced
2 peaches, sliced
1 orange, peeled and sectioned
½ cup strawberries, sliced
1 tablespoon lemon juice

Place tapioca, sugar and ½ the water in a medium saucepan over medium heat. Bring to a boil. Simmer, uncovered, until cooked, about 20 minutes. Pour into a medium bowl; stir in orange juice and remaining water. Allow to cool. Stir again and chill in the refrigerator. Stir in fruits and lemon juice. Makes 4 to 6 servings.

Apricot Milk Shake   ★ W M E A

3 cups apricots, measured then soaked

2 cups water in which apricots were soaked
2 cups milk substitute

Place all ingredients in a blender or food processor fitted with a steel blade. Process until smooth and creamy. Pour into a pitcher. Refrigerate until chilled. Makes 4 to 6 servings.

Beverages

Tea with Fresh Mint 

1 tea bag   2½ cups boiling water
2 mint sprigs

Place tea bag and mint sprigs in a teapot. Add boiling water; brew 5 minutes. Stir and serve. Makes 2 to 4 servings.

Gingerroot Tea 

1 (2-inch) gingerroot piece,   4 cloves
    peeled and chopped   3¾ cups water
2½ tablespoons honey

Peel the gingerroot and chop it coarsely. Place gingerroot, honey, cloves and water in a saucepan. Bring to a boil; reduce heat. Cover and simmer 25 minutes. Remove lid and simmer 15 minutes. Strain and serve hot or cold. Makes 4 servings.

Tip

For weaker tea use less gingerroot.

Peanut Milk 

¾ cup shelled peanuts   2 teaspoons honey or to taste
2½ cups water

Place peanuts, water and honey in a blender or food processor fitted with a steel blade. Process until thoroughly blended. Pour into a pitcher. Refrigerate until chilled. Stir before serving. Makes 4 servings.

Rice Tea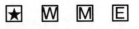

2 tablespoons uncooked white rice   3¾ cups boiling water

Place the rice in a small, heavy skillet over medium heat. Heat until rice turns dark brown, stirring constantly. Pour into a small saucepan; add boiling water. Simmer, uncovered, 1 minute. Strain and serve. Makes 3 to 4 servings.

Sweet Yogurt Drink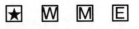

½ cup unflavored yogurt   2 tablespoons honey
1½ cups ice-cold water

Place ingredients in a blender or food processor fitted with a steel blade. Process until smooth and creamy. Pour into a pitcher. Refrigerate until chilled. Makes 2 servings.

Tomato Cocktail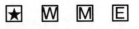

3¼ cups tomato juice   ½ cup unsweetened apple juice
⅔ cup goat's milk yogurt   Mint leaves

Place tomato juice, yogurt and apple juice in a blender or food processor fitted with a steel blade. Process until thoroughly blended. Pour into a pitcher. Refrigerate until chilled. Stir before serving. Garnish with mint leaves. Makes 6 servings.

Mixed Fruit Cocktail

4 tablespoons chopped fresh fruit (for example, peaches, grapes, banana)   2½ cups unsweetened grape juice

Place fruit in a medium bowl. Pour grape juice over. Mix well. Refrigerate until chilled. Makes 4 servings.

Appetizers

Avocado Dip   Ⓜ Ⓜ Ⓔ

1 lemon
1 garlic clove, crushed
2 tomatoes, peeled, seeded
and chopped
Salt and pepper to taste
2 avocados
6 tablespoons olive oil

Crudités:
4 medium carrots, sliced into
long strips

4 celery stalks, sliced into
long strips
½ medium cucumber, sliced
into long strips
1 medium green bell pepper,
sliced into long strips
1 medium red bell pepper,
sliced into long strips
½ small cauliflower, broken
into flowerets

Peel lemon; juice. Place lemon juice, peel, garlic, tomatoes and
seasoning in a blender or food processor fitted with a steel blade.
Process until well blended. Add avocados to blender or food processor; process until pureed. With motor running, gradually add
olive oil in a slow, steady stream. Process until mixture is creamy
and pale green.

Pour dip into a bowl. Place the bowl in the middle of a large
serving dish and arrange vegetables in a circle around bowl. Makes
4 to 6 servings.

Eggplant Puree   Ⓜ Ⓜ Ⓔ

2 large eggplants
1 garlic clove, crushed, if
desired
2 teaspoons lemon juice
2 tablespoons sunflower oil

Salt and pepper to taste
Chopped fresh parsley
Few ripe olives
Few lemon wedges

Preheat broiler. Broil eggplants 5 inches from heat, turning
occasionally, 15 to 25 minutes, until skins are black and blistered.
Remove eggplants from broiler. Put under cold running water and
pull off skins. Place eggplants in a sieve and press down hard with a

---

Curried Apple & Carrot Soup (*above and center*, see page 48); Eggplant
Puree (*below*)
OVERLEAF: Green & White Salad (*top left*, see page 52); Marinated Fried
Tofu (*below left*, see page 56); Mushrooms with Cilantro (*center*, see
page 55); Eggplant & Buckwheat Pasta (*right*, see page 58)

wooden spoon to remove the juice. Place eggplant in a blender or food processor fitted with a steel blade. Add garlic (if desired) and lemon juice. With motor running gradually add sunflower oil in a slow, steady stream. Process until smooth and creamy. Season with salt and pepper. Garnish with parsley, ripe olives and lemon wedges. Makes 4 servings.

Dolmades   ★ W M E

12 grape leaves or Savoy
   cabbage leaves
½ lb. ground veal or lean beef
⅓ cup cooked rice
1 garlic clove, crushed

½ teaspoon mint, chopped
1 teaspoon chopped parsley
1 pinch ground cinnamon
1 tablespoon olive oil
Salt and pepper to taste

Preheat oven to 350F (175C).
   Parboil the grape leaves in boiling water 2 minutes. If using cabbage leaves, parboil 5 minutes. Drain carefully, drape on the sides of a colander and allow to cool.
   Place the ground meat in a medium bowl, add the rice, garlic, mint, parsley and cinnamon. Mix well. Add olive oil; mix again. Add salt and pepper.
   Spread out cooled leaves on a flat surface. Divide meat mixture into 12 portions. Place each in the middle of a leaf. Wrap leaf around the meat mixture. Put leaves in a shallow baking dish. Pour a little water into the bottom of the dish and cover tightly with lid or foil. Bake for 1 hour. Makes 6 servings as an appetizer, 3 as an entree.

Mary's Salmon Delight ★ W M E A

½ lb. salmon steak or fillet
5 black peppercorns
2 tablespoons kosher margarine
4 celery stalks, sliced
¼ cup crushed rice cakes

Sauce:
1 tablespoon kosher margarine
1 tablespoon soy flour
6 tablespoons milk substitute
Salt and pepper to taste

Preheat oven to 400F (205C).
   Place salmon and peppercorns in a baking dish. Add enough water to cover. Poach salmon until it turns from transparent to opaque, about 10 minutes. Melt margarine in a small saucepan over medium heat. Add celery; sauté 3 to 4 minutes. Drain salmon, discarding liquid and peppercorns. Flake salmon into bite-sized pieces. Place flaked salmon in a shallow baking dish and sprinkle celery on top. Prepare sauce. Pour sauce over salmon and celery. Top with crushed rice cakes. Bake in preheated oven until hot, 10 to 15 minutes. Makes 6 servings. ➡

Dolmades (*above*); Mary's Salmon Delight (*below*)

Sauce:
Melt kosher margarine in a small saucepan over low heat. Add flour and stir well. Simmer 2 minutes. Heat milk substitute in a very small saucepan until warm. Add warmed milk substitute to flour mixture, stirring continuously. Increase heat. Bring mixture to a boil, then reduce heat and simmer 2 minutes. Add salt and pepper.

Turkey Liver Pâté

½ cup kosher margarine
½ lb. turkey livers, chopped
1 celery stalk, finely chopped

1 large garlic clove, crushed
½ teaspoon Italian seasoning
Salt and pepper to taste

Place 2 tablespoons margarine in a medium skillet over medium heat. Add livers and celery. Sauté 3 minutes. Add garlic, Italian seasoning, salt and pepper and cook 15 minutes, stirring occasionally. Melt remaining margarine in pan over low heat.

Pour liver mixture into blender or food processor fitted with a steel blade. Add melted margarine. Process until pureed. Spoon pâté mixture into small serving bowl and cover with foil. Refrigerate until chilled, about 2 hours. Makes 2 servings.

Chicken Liver Salad

⅔ cup dried navy or lima beans
½ lb. chicken livers
1 tablespoon olive oil
2 celery stalks, finely chopped
2 small tomatoes, peeled,
   seeded and sliced
Toasted sesame seeds

Apple-Juice Dressing:
2 tablespoons olive oil
1 tablespoon unsweetened
   apple juice
2 tablespoons wheat-free
   tamari sauce
Pepper to taste

Soak the beans overnight in enough water to cover by 2 inches. Drain. Add drained beans to a medium saucepan. Add enough water to cover by 2 inches. Boil until tender, 1½ hours. Allow to cool.

Slice livers into thin strips. Heat oil in a medium skillet and sauté liver strips gently for a few minutes. Remove from pan and drain on paper towels. Allow to cool to room temperature. Drain beans and put them in a large serving bowl. Add celery, tomatoes and livers. Prepare dressing. Pour over salad and toss well. Chill. Before serving, toss again and garnish with sesame seeds. Makes 4 servings as an appetizer, 2 as an entree.

Dressing:
Combine olive oil, apple juice, tamari sauce and pepper in a small bowl.

Soups

Curried Parsnip Soup

4 medium parsnips
6 tablespoons kosher margarine
1 medium onion, chopped
1 garlic clove, crushed
3 tablespoons rice flour

2 tablespoons wheat-free curry
  powder
6 cups hot beef stock (see
  page 90)
Salt and pepper to taste

Peel and slice parsnips. Melt margarine in a medium, heavy saucepan over low heat. Add parsnips, onion and garlic. Cover pan and cook 10 minutes, until vegetables are limp, stirring frequently. Do not brown vegetables. Add rice flour and curry powder, stirring continuously. Gradually pour in beef stock. Increase heat. Bring to a boil. Reduce heat and simmer until parsnips are fork tender, about 20 minutes. In a blender or food processor fitted with a steel blade, puree soup in batches. Return mixture to pan; add salt and pepper. Heat through. Makes 6 to 8 servings.

Celery Soup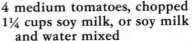

⅔ cup chopped celery
⅔ cup soy milk
1¼ cups water

3 tablespoons lentils
1 garlic clove, crushed
Salt and pepper to taste

Place celery, milk, water, lentils and garlic in a medium saucepan. Bring to a boil. Reduce heat and simmer 5 to 10 minutes until the ingredients are soft enough to process in a blender. In a blender or food processor fitted with a steel blade, puree soup in batches. Return mixture to pan; add salt and pepper. Heat through. Makes 2 servings.

Spinach & Tomato Soup

1¼ cups beef or Tongue Stock
(see page 77)
1 cup packed fresh spinach or
  beet leaves and stems,
  chopped

4 medium tomatoes, chopped
1¼ cups soy milk, or soy milk
  and water mixed
2 teaspoons tomato paste
Freshly ground black pepper

Prepare stock. Place stock, spinach or beet leaves and stems, soy milk or soy milk and water into a medium saucepan. Bring to a boil. Reduce heat and simmer until heated through. In a blender or food processor fitted with a steel blade, puree soup in batches. Return mixture to pan; add tomato paste and pepper. Heat through. Makes 4 servings.

Salsify & Apple Soup   ★ Ⓜ Ⓜ Ⓔ Ⓐ

½ lb. salsify or carrots
1 Golden Delicious apple
1 tablespoon yellow split peas
1¼ cups water

⅔ cup soy milk
Salt and pepper to taste
Watercress sprigs

Peel the salsify or carrots. Cut into 2 to 3 inch pieces. Core and quarter the apple. Do not peel; skin will increase fiber content of soup. Place salsify or carrots, apple and split peas in a medium saucepan. Add water and bring to a boil. Reduce heat and cover. Simmer 30 to 40 minutes, until the salsify and peas are soft enough to be processed in a blender. In a blender or food processor fitted with a steel blade, puree soup in batches. Return mixture to pan; add soy milk, salt and pepper. Heat through. Garnish with watercress. Makes 2 servings.

Curried Apple & Carrot Soup   ★ Ⓜ Ⓜ Ⓔ

See photograph, page 41

1 Golden Delicious apple
1 tablespoon soybean oil
½ lb. carrots, sliced into thin
   rounds
1 teaspoon wheat-free curry
   powder

1 tablespoon brown-rice miso
2½ cups hot water
Salt and pepper
Finely chopped chives

Core and quarter apple. Do not peel; skin will increase fiber content of soup. Heat oil in a medium saucepan over medium-low heat; add carrots and apple. Reduce heat. Cook in their own juices over low heat 30 minutes, shaking the pan occasionally to prevent sticking. Stir in curry powder and cook several minutes. In a medium bowl, mix the miso and hot water; add to mixture in pan. In a blender or food processor fitted with a steel blade, puree soup in batches. Return mixture to pan; add salt and pepper. Heat through. Do not allow the soup to boil; the miso will curdle. Garnish with chopped chives. Makes 2 to 3 servings.

Cream of Artichoke Soup ★ Ⓦ Ⓜ ⒺⒶ

½ lb. Jerusalem artichokes
3 tablespoons yellow split peas
2½ cups water

Salt and pepper to taste
Dash of paprika
Parsley sprigs

Peel artichokes. Place artichokes, split peas and enough water to cover in a medium saucepan; bring to a boil. Skim off foam, reduce heat. Cover and simmer for 30 to 40 minutes, until split peas are soft enough to be processed in a blender and the artichokes are fork tender.

In a blender or food processor fitted with a steel blade, puree soup in batches. Return mixture to pan; add salt and pepper. Heat through. Garnish with paprika and parsley. Makes 2 to 3 servings.

Salads

Bean Salad ★ Ⓦ Ⓜ Ⓔ

½ cup dried red kidney beans
½ cup lima beans
¼ lb. green beans, chopped
2 tablespoons parsley, chopped
1 tablespoon chives, chopped

Dressing:
2 tablespoons unsweetened
  apple juice
2 tablespoons olive oil
Pinch of sugar
Salt and pepper to taste

Place kidney beans and lima beans in separate saucepans. Add enough water to cover by 2 inches. Soak beans separately overnight. Boil soaked beans separately, in enough water to cover by 2 inches until tender, 1½ hours. Drain. In a medium saucepan, bring 1 inch of water to a boil. Add green beans. Boil until tender, 10 minutes. Drain. Cool beans slightly. Prepare dressing. In a large bowl, combine drained beans and dressing. Toss well. Cover and refrigerate until chilled. Stir in parsley and chives just before serving. Makes 6 servings.

Dressing:
In a medium bowl combine apple juice, olive oil, sugar, salt and pepper. Beat until slightly thickened.

Bean & Pepper Salad   ★ Ⓜ Ⓜ Ⓔ Ⓐ

1 cup black-eyed peas
1 medium red bell pepper,
  sliced into thin strips
1 yellow or green bell pepper,
  sliced into thin strips
1 tablespoon chopped parsley

Dressing:
6 tablespoons olive oil
2 tablespoons unsweetened
  apple juice
Pinch of wheat-free dry
  mustard
Freshly ground black pepper

Place peas in a medium saucepan. Add enough water to cover by 2 inches. Bring to a boil; reduce heat and simmer until tender, about 45 minutes. Prepare dressing. Drain peas. Place peas in a medium bowl and add dressing. Toss well. Cover and refrigerate until chilled. Just before serving, add the green and red bell peppers and parsley. Toss again. Makes 6 servings.

Dressing:
In a medium bowl, combine olive oil, apple juice, dry mustard and pepper. Beat until slightly thickened.

Apple & Spinach Salad   Ⓜ Ⓜ Ⓔ

2 cups packed spinach
2 cups cored and diced Red
  Delicious apples
1 cup thinly sliced onion
1 cup walnuts, chopped and
  toasted   ·

Dressing:
2 tablespoons lemon juice
1 tablespoon wheat-free
  prepared mustard
½ teaspoon sugar
⅔ cup olive oil
Salt and pepper to taste

Wash, trim and pat dry spinach. Tear into small pieces. In a large bowl mix together spinach, apple, onion and walnuts. Prepare dressing. Add dressing to salad and toss well. Makes 6 servings.

Dressing:
Combine lemon juice, mustard and sugar in a medium bowl. Add olive oil in a stream, whisking continuously. Whisk in salt and pepper.

Carrot & Beet Salad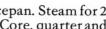

2 medium carrots, grated
2 tablespoons shredded coconut
1 tablespoon golden raisins

2 or 3 small cooked beets,
sliced into rounds

Place carrots, coconut and raisins in a medium bowl. Mix well. Arrange beets around edges of 2 medium-sized plates. Place carrot mixture in middle of beets. Makes 2 servings.

Zucchini & Apple Salad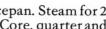

2 medium zucchini, cut into
sticks
1 Granny Smith apple
¼ cup golden raisins

Pinch of Italian seasoning
Salt and pepper to taste
¼ cup unsweetened apple juice

Place zucchini and ¼ cup water in a medium saucepan. Steam for 2 to 3 minutes. Cool to room temperature. Drain. Core, quarter and slice apple. Do not peel. Place drained zucchini, apple and raisins in a medium bowl. Stir until combined well. Sprinkle Italian seasoning, salt and pepper over mixture. Add apple juice. Toss well.

Marinate for 15 to 30 minutes, tossing occasionally. Makes 2 servings.

Curried Chicken Salad

1 small cooked chicken, cut
into small pieces
1 celery heart, shredded
1 large lettuce, shredded
2 tablespoons vinegar
Salt and pepper to taste

Dressing:
⅔ cup Egg-Free Mayonnaise
(see page 93)
1 teaspoon wheat-free curry
powder
1 tablespoon parsley, chopped
1 garlic clove, crushed
½ teaspoon paprika

Place chicken, celery and lettuce in a large bowl. Add vinegar and mix. Add salt and pepper and mix well. Prepare dressing. Place salad in a salad bowl and add dressing. Toss well. Makes 6 servings.

Dressing:
Place all ingredients in a medium bowl. Mix thoroughly.

Marinated Pea & Cauliflower Salad ★ Ⓜ Ⓜ Ⓔ Ⓐ

2 (10-oz.) pkgs. frozen green peas
½ cauliflower, broken into flowerets
½ cup pimento-stuffed green olives

2 tablespoons grated gingerroot
1 cup olive oil
¼ teaspoon ground nutmeg
Salt and pepper to taste
2 tablespoons chopped parsley

Place peas, cauliflowerets, olives, gingerroot, olive oil, nutmeg, salt and pepper in a saucepan with a tight-fitting lid. Bring to a boil; turn off heat. Leave with lid on for 5 to 6 minutes. Pour into a medium bowl. Cover and refrigerate 3 to 4 hours. Bring to room temperature. Fold in the parsley just before serving. Makes 6 servings.

Green & White Salad ★ Ⓜ Ⓜ Ⓔ Ⓐ

See photograph, page 42

½ head iceberg lettuce, chopped
4 cups bean sprouts
1 kiwifruit, peeled and sliced
½ Granny Smith apple, cored and chopped

¼ green bell pepper, chopped
1 (4-inch) cucumber, chopped
Apple-Juice Dressing (see page 50)

Arrange lettuce in the bottom of a large shallow dish. If you are using a rectangular dish, halve the total quantity and put half the bean sprouts across each end. If you are using a round dish, put the bean sprouts around the perimeter of the dish. Place kiwifruit slices in center of the dish. Place apple, bell pepper and cucumber between the kiwifruit and bean sprouts. Cover and refrigerate. Prepare Apple-Juice Dressing (see page 50). Sprinkle dressing on salad. Makes 6 servings.

Tomato & Kiwifruit Salad ★ Ⓜ Ⓜ Ⓔ

3 to 4 tomatoes, sliced in rounds
4 kiwifruit, peeled and sliced in rounds

2 tablespoons unsweetened apple juice
2 tablespoons olive oil
Pinch of sugar
Salt and pepper to taste

Place tomatoes and kiwifruit in a medium serving bowl. In a separate bowl combine apple juice, olive oil and sugar. Add salt and pepper. Pour apple juice mixture over tomatoes and kiwifruit. Mix gently. Makes 4 servings.

Oriental Banana Salad   ★ W M E

1 medium banana, sliced
Pinch of sugar
Pinch of salt
Freshly ground black pepper

Pinch of ground cumin
Pinch of red (cayenne) pepper
Dash of unsweetened apple
  juice

Place all ingredients in a medium bowl. Toss thoroughly. Makes 1 serving.

Vegetables

Red Cabbage

1 medium head red cabbage	1 medium Granny Smith apple,
2 tablespoons kosher margarine	peeled and chopped
1 teaspoon sugar	6 to 8 black peppercorns
	1 cup unsweetened apple juice
	⅓ cup golden raisins

Discard central stalk and outer leaves of cabbage. Shred the rest.

Melt margarine in a large pan over low heat. Add cabbage; cook until margarine has been absorbed. Add sugar, apple and peppercorns. Pour in apple juice and bring to a boil. Reduce heat and cover. Simmer 45 minutes. Add golden raisins and simmer 15 minutes. Serve hot or cold. Makes 6 servings.

Baked Zucchini ★ Ⓜ Ⓜ Ⓔ

4 small or 2 large zucchini	Salt and pepper to taste
6 to 8 medium tomatoes	Pinch of dried leaf oregano
1 garlic clove, crushed	Pinch of dried leaf basil

Preheat oven to 375F (190C).

Cut zucchini in half lengthwise. Scoop out, leaving a ¼-inch shell and discarding centers. Arrange zucchini shells in a shallow baking dish. Chop tomatoes and save juice. In a medium bowl, mix tomatoes and juice, garlic, salt, pepper, oregano and basil. Pour mixture into zucchini shells, letting any extra spill over into dish. Bake uncovered until bubbling, about 30 minutes. Makes 4 servings.

Mushrooms with Cilantro ★ Ⓦ Ⓜ Ⓔ Ⓐ
See photograph, page 43

1 tablespoon kosher margarine	2 teaspoons cilantro
½ lb. mushrooms	leaves, finely chopped
	¼ teaspoon ground coriander

Melt margarine in a medium skillet. Add mushrooms and cilantro; sauté until liquid disappears. Stir in coriander. Makes 2 servings.

Stir-Fried Mixed Vegetables ★ Ⓦ Ⓜ Ⓔ Ⓐ

3 tablespoons sunflower oil	½ red bell pepper, chopped
1 garlic clove, crushed	1 large carrot, thinly sliced on
1 (1-inch) gingerroot, finely	the diagonal
chopped	¼ cauliflower, broken into
Salt and black pepper to taste	flowerets
½ green bell pepper, chopped	1½ cups bean sprouts

Heat oil in a large skillet. Add garlic, gingerroot, salt and pepper; stir-fry 1 minute. Add bell peppers, carrot and cauliflower; stir-fry 4 minutes. Add bean sprouts; stir-fry 4 minutes. Pour vegetables into warm serving dish and serve immediately. Makes 2 to 3 servings.

Vegetarian Dishes

See photograph, page 42

Marinated Fried Tofu ★ W M E A

10 oz. firm tofu
2 tablespoons wheat-free
  tamari sauce

2 garlic cloves, crushed
Millet flour
Sunflower oil

Cut tofu into ½-inch-thick slices. Mix the tamari and garlic in a medium bowl and add tofu. Marinate 1 to 2 hours.

Remove tofu from marinade and coat tofu slices with millet flour. Heat ½ inch oil in a medium skillet. Fry tofu in batches until golden brown, turning once. Makes 2 to 4 servings.

Chinese-Style Tofu ★ W M E A

1 teaspoon arrowroot or
  cornstarch
¼ cup water
2 tablespoons sunflower oil
1 green chili pepper, cut into
  thin strips
1 red bell pepper, cut into
  thin strips

¼ teaspoon salt
½ lb. firm tofu, cut into
  1-inch cubes
1 tablespoon wheat-free tamari
  sauce
¼ cup cilantro, finely
  chopped

Mix arrowroot and water in a cup. Heat oil in a heavy medium skillet. Add chili, red pepper and salt. Stir-fry 30 seconds. Reduce heat and add the tofu, stirring gently. Add tamari and arrowroot mixture. Stir carefully until sauce thickens.

Stir in cilantro, serve immediately. Makes 2 servings.

Lima-Bean Curry

½ lb. dried lima beans
1 teaspoon cumin seeds
3 tablespoons vegetable oil
1 onion, chopped
2 tablespoons chopped
  gingerroot
2 garlic cloves, crushed
1 teaspoon ground cumin
1 chili pepper, chopped

1 teaspoon ground coriander
½ teaspoon turmeric
4 whole cloves
1 lb. tomatoes, peeled and
  chopped
1¼ cups water
2 teaspoons Garam Masala
  (see page 30)
Salt and pepper to taste

Soak beans in water overnight. Drain and rinse. Place beans and enough water to cover them in a medium saucepan. Bring to a boil. Reduce heat. Cover and simmer until tender, about 1½ hours. Drain, set aside.

Dry roast the cumin seeds in a small heavy saucepan until toasted. Set aside.

Heat oil in a medium skillet. Add onions; sauté until soft. Add gingerroot and garlic; cook 2 minutes. Add cumin, chili, coriander, tumeric, cloves, tomatoes and water. Cook 15 minutes. Stir in garam masala, salt and pepper. Makes 4 servings.

Eggplant Supper

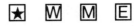

2 lbs. eggplant, sliced
Salt
¾ cup olive oil
2 heads chicory, chopped
1 lb. tomatoes, skinned, seeded
  and sliced (1½ cups)
2 garlic cloves, crushed

Salt and pepper to taste
1¼ cup goat's milk yogurt
⅔ cup fresh goat's milk cheese
Kosher margarine
½ cup shredded goat's milk
  Cheddar cheese

Preheat oven to 375F (190C).

Sprinkle eggplant with salt; leave 30 minutes. Rinse and drain. Heat ½ cup of oil in a large skillet and fry eggplant slices until golden brown on both sides. Set aside. Add chicory; cook over low heat in remaining oil for 15 minutes. Remove from heat; add tomatoes, garlic, salt and pepper. Mix well and set aside. Combine yogurt with fresh goat's cheese in a small bowl. Mix well.

Grease an ovenproof dish with margarine. Place one-third of the eggplant in the bottom, then one-third of the tomato mixture, then one-third of the yogurt mixture. Continue layering until all the ingredients have been used. Sprinkle Cheddar cheese on top. Bake for 30 minutes. Makes 4 servings.

See photograph, page 43

Eggplant & Buckwheat Pasta Ⓜ Ⓜ Ⓔ

1 eggplant, sliced
Salt
3 tablespoons sunflower oil
1 garlic clove, crushed
1 onion, sliced
1 teaspoon dried leaf oregano

1 small green bell pepper,
  sliced
2 medium tomatoes
Salt and pepper to taste
6 oz. buckwheat pasta, cooked
  and kept warm
3 oz. feta cheese

Sprinkle eggplant with salt; leave 30 minutes. Rinse and drain. Heat oil in a large skillet; add garlic and onion. Sauté 5 minutes. Add eggplant, oregano, bell pepper and tomatoes. Reduce heat; simmer 15 minutes. Add salt and pepper. Place pasta in warm serving dish. Pour eggplant mixture into middle of pasta. Crumble feta cheese over top. Makes 2 servings.

Turmeric Rice ★ Ⓜ Ⓜ Ⓔ

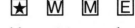

1¾ cups uncooked brown rice
Pinch of salt
½ teaspoon powdered turmeric
4½ cups boiling water

½ cup golden raisins, soaked
  3 to 4 hours in unsweetened
  apple juice, if desired

Place rice in a large saucepan. Add salt and turmeric. Pour in boiling water; bring mixture to a boil. Stir well, cover with a tight-fitting lid and simmer for about 35 minutes or until all the water is absorbed and the rice is cooked. Stir in golden raisins (if desired) and serve. Makes 6 servings.

Stuffed Peppers ★ Ⓜ Ⓜ Ⓔ

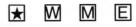

3 green bell peppers
1 tablespoon soy oil
4 tomatoes, chopped
Salt and black pepper to taste

2 tablespoons chopped fresh
  basil
1½ cups cooked brown rice

With a sharp knife, cut off bell pepper tops to make lids. Carefully remove the seeds and cores. Steam pepper shells and lids 7 to 10 minutes, until they are cooked crisp-tender. Keep warm. Heat oil in a large skillet. Add tomatoes, salt, pepper and basil; sauté until tomatoes are soft. Stir cooked rice into tomato mixture. Cook until heated through.

Place each pepper on a warm serving plate. Spoon rice-and-tomato mixture into peppers and replace lids. Serve immediately. Makes 3 servings.

Rice Tabbouleh

2¼ cups cooked brown rice
1 bunch green onions, chopped
½ cup chopped parsley
½ cup chopped mint

Juice from 1 lemon
3 tomatoes, chopped
3 tablespoons olive oil
Salt and pepper to taste

Place all ingredients except salt and pepper in a large bowl. Mix thoroughly; add salt and pepper. Makes 4 servings.

Vegetarian Paella

2 eggplants, diced
Salt
2 tablespoons sunflower oil
2 garlic cloves, crushed
2 onions, chopped
3 bay leaves
½ red bell pepper, sliced

½ green bell pepper, sliced
6 tomatoes, chopped
½ lb small mushrooms
3 cups cooked brown rice
6 oz. mixed nuts, chopped
  and toasted
Juice of 1 lemon

Sprinkle eggplants with salt; place in a strainer and drain 30 minutes. Rinse; set aside. Heat oil in a large skillet. Add garlic, onions and bay leaves; sauté 5 minutes. Add eggplants, bell peppers, tomatoes and mushrooms. Cook 5 to 10 minutes, until vegetables are tender. Add rice, nuts and lemon juice. Simmer until heated through. Serve immediately. Makes 4 servings.

Variation:
Legumes such as kidney beans or azuki beans can be substituted for chopped nuts.

Vegetable Curry   ★ W M E

¾ cup yellow split peas
1¼ cups water or brown-rice
  miso stock
⅓ cauliflower broken into
  flowerets
2 medium carrots, chopped
1 medium rutabaga, chopped
½ teaspoon wheat-free curry
  powder

2 teaspoons Garam Masala
  (see page 30)
2 teaspoons tomato paste
2 tablespoons sunflower oil
2 tomatoes, chopped
1 cup fresh or ½ (10-oz.) pkg.
  frozen green peas
Salt and pepper to taste

Place split peas in a medium saucepan with enough water to cover. Soak overnight. Drain and rinse. Place in a medium saucepan with 1¼ cups of water or miso stock. Bring to a boil; reduce heat and simmer until split peas are tender, about ½ hour. Steam cauliflower, carrots and rutabaga until crisp-tender, about 5 minutes. Drain; save cooking water. Pour split peas and liquid they were cooked in into a blender or food processor fitted with a steel blade. Process until pureed. Add curry powder, garam masala and tomato paste; process until mixture has consistency of cream soup. Add reserved vegetable cooking water to achieve consistency if necessary; set puree aside.

Heat oil in a large skillet. Add drained vegetables; sauté until heated through. Add tomatoes and peas; cook 2 to 3 minutes, stirring frequently. Add puree, salt and pepper. Bring to a boil. Reduce heat; simmer 5 minutes. Makes 2 servings.

Indian Millet
with Yellow Split Peas   ★ W M E A

½ cup yellow split peas
1 cup whole millet
1 tablespoon sunflower oil
½ teaspoon cumin seeds
½ teaspoon mustard seeds
2 celery stalks, finely chopped
1 garlic clove, crushed

½ teaspoon ground turmeric
½ teaspoon ground cumin
1 teaspoon ground coriander
⅛ teaspoon red (cayenne)
  pepper
2 cups water
2 tablespoons chopped parsley

Place split peas in a medium saucepan with enough water to cover. Soak overnight. Drain and rinse. Dry roast millet in a heavy skillet over medium heat until it starts to turn light brown. Heat oil in a medium saucepan. Add cumin seeds, mustard seeds, celery and garlic; sauté 2 to 3 minutes. Add split peas, toasted millet and spices. Sauté 2 minutes. Add 2 cups water and bring to a boil. Cover; reduce heat. Simmer until peas are tender, adding more boiling water if mixture begins drying out. Turn off heat and leave saucepan, covered, 15 minutes. Remove lid, stir mixture quickly with a fork. Garnish with parsley. Makes 4 servings.

Split-Pea Cutlets with Apple Rings

1¾ cups yellow split peas
2 cups water
2 tablespoons kosher margarine
1 large onion, peeled and chopped, or 1 celery stalk, chopped
½ teaspoon rubbed sage
⅛ teaspoon ground cloves
1 egg
Salt and pepper to taste

Rice flour
1 egg, beaten
Millet flakes
Sunflower oil

Apple Rings:
2 medium Granny Smith apples, peeled and cored
2 tablespoons kosher margarine
2 tablespoons sunflower oil

Place split peas in a medium saucepan with enough water to cover. Soak overnight. Drain and rinse. Place in a medium saucepan with 2 cups water and cook until split peas are tender and all liquid has been absorbed. If peas are cooked before water has been absorbed, drain the beans and dry them by stirring over a low heat. Melt margarine in a medium skillet. Add onion or celery. Sauté 5 minutes. Add split peas, sage, cloves and egg. Mix well, mashing split peas with a spoon. Season with salt and pepper. Allow to cool. Dust a cutting board or counter with rice flour. Pour mixture on board or counter and shape into 12 cutlets. Dip each cutlet into beaten egg, then coat evenly with millet flakes. Heat ½ inch oil in medium skillet. Fry cutlets until golden brown and cooked through. Drain on paper towels. Keep warm. Prepare Apple Rings. Serve cutlets with Apple Rings. Makes 6 servings.

Apple Rings:
Slice apples into thin rings. Heat the margarine and oil in a medium skillet. Add apple rings; sauté about 2 minutes on each side until lightly browned. Drain on paper towels.

Colorful Lentils

¼ cup olive oil
3 garlic cloves, crushed
4 carrots, chopped
1 green bell pepper, chopped
1 red bell pepper, chopped
1 teaspoon dried leaf basil
3 celery stalks, chopped

1 tablespoon brown-rice miso
3¾ cups hot water
1½ lbs. tomatoes, peeled, seeded and chopped
10 oz. lentils (about 1½ cups)
Salt and black pepper to taste
2 tablespoons chopped parsley

Heat oil in a large saucepan. Add garlic, carrots, bell peppers, basil and celery. Cook until ingredients are soft, 5 to 10 minutes. In a medium bowl, mix the miso with hot water; add to vegetable mixture. Stir in tomatoes, lentils, salt and pepper.

Simmer until lentils are tender, about 1 hour. Garnish with parsley. Makes 4 servings as an entree, 6 as a side dish.

Lentil Rissoles

8 oz. lentils (about 1¼ cups)
1¼ cups water
2 tablespoons sunflower oil
1 celery stalk, chopped
1 large garlic clove, crushed
1 small green bell pepper, chopped
1 teaspoon ground turmeric
1 teaspoon ground coriander
1 teaspoon ground cumin
¼ teaspoon chili powder
Salt and black pepper to taste
Rice flour or millet flour
Sunflower oil

Place lentils in a large saucepan with 1¼ cups water. Bring to a boil. Reduce heat and simmer until lentils are tender and have absorbed all the liquid, about 1 hour.

Heat oil in a medium skillet. Add celery, garlic and bell pepper; cook 5 minutes. Stir in turmeric, coriander, cumin and chili powder; cook 2 minutes. Add mixture to lentils. Stir well; add salt and pepper. Allow to cool.

Mold mixture into small half-circles. Coat evenly with rice flour or millet flour. Heat ½-inch oil in a medium skillet. Add half-circles in batches; fry until browned and cooked through. Drain on paper towels. Serve hot or cold. Makes 4 servings.

Snacks

See photograph, page 92

Cucumber Dip ★ W M E A

⅔ cup goat's milk yogurt
½ large cucumber, diced
Salt and pepper to taste

2 teaspoons mint, finely
  chopped

Place yogurt and diced cucumber in a blender or food processor fitted with a steel blade. Process until pureed. Add salt and pepper; fold in mint. Pour into a bowl. Cover and refrigerate until chilled, about 2 hours. Makes 1 cup.

Cheese Dip ★ W M E A

⅔ cup goat's milk yogurt
⅔ cup soft goat's cheese
4 garlic cloves, crushed

½ teaspoon paprika or red
  (cayenne) pepper

Place yogurt, cheese and garlic in a blender or food processor fitted with a steel blade. Process until smooth. Pour into a bowl. Cover and refrigerate until chilled, about 2 hours. Garnish with paprika or red pepper. Makes about 1⅓ cups.

See photograph, page 92

Tofu Spread ★ W M E

10 oz. tofu
1 tablespoon wheat-free
  tamari sauce
1 tablespoon tomato paste
1 garlic clove, crushed

1 teaspoon chopped fresh
  basil, or ⅓ teaspoon dried
  leaf basil
⅛ teaspoon salt
⅛ teaspoon pepper

Place all ingredients in a blender or food processor fitted with a steel blade. Process until smooth. Makes about 2 cups.

Salad Dip ☒ Ⓦ Ⓜ Ⓔ

3 garlic cloves
2 celery stalks, chopped
1 green bell pepper, chopped
½ teaspoon dried leaf basil
1 (2-inch) cucumber piece,
  peeled and diced

2 teaspoons olive oil
5 oz. fresh goat's cheese
2 tomatoes, peeled, seeded
  and sliced
Salt and pepper to taste

Place garlic, celery and bell pepper in a medium saucepan. Add just enough water to cover vegetables. Bring to a boil; reduce heat and simmer 8 minutes. Drain; stir in basil. Cool to room temperature.

Place cooled vegetables in a blender or food processor fitted with a steel blade. Add cucumber, olive oil, goat's cheese and tomatoes. Process until pureed. Add salt and pepper. Pour into a bowl. Cover and refrigerate until chilled, about 2 hours. Makes about 2 cups.

See photograph, page 92

Bean & Apple Dip ☒ Ⓦ Ⓜ Ⓔ

3 cups red kidney beans,
  pre-soaked
1 tablespoon tomato juice
1 medium Granny Smith apple,
  chopped

2 tablespoons goat's milk
  yogurt
¼ teaspoon salt
Freshly ground pepper
Chopped fresh chives

Place beans, tomato juice, apple, yogurt, salt and pepper in a blender or food processor fitted with a steel blade. Process until pureed. Garnish with chives. Makes about 4 cups.

See photograph, page 92

Deep-Fried Mung Beans ☒ Ⓦ Ⓜ Ⓔ Ⓐ

¼ cup mung beans
Sunflower oil
Salt and pepper to taste

Place beans in a medium saucepan with enough water to cover. Soak 24 hours. Drain and rinse. Pat dry with paper towel. Line a basket with more paper towels. Heat 3 inches of oil in a deep saucepan over medium heat. When oil is hot, add half of dried beans. Cook until browned and crisp, about 1½ minutes. Remove with a slotted spoon. Drain on paper towels. Repeat with remaining beans. Season beans with salt and pepper. Serve hot or cold. Makes 2 servings.

Garbanzo-Bean Pancake ★ W M E A
with Savory Pancake Filling

See photograph, page 70

¼ cup garbanzo-bean flour
⅓ cup water
Pinch of turmeric
Pinch of salt
Pinch of red (cayenne) pepper
1 tablespoon sunflower oil

Savory Pancake Filling:
1 tablespoon sunflower oil

1 Granny Smith apple, cored
and chopped
1 celery stalk, sliced
1½ tablespoons green bell
pepper, chopped
2 tablespoons cold Deep-Fried
Mung Beans (see page 64)
1 tomato, chopped
1½ tablespoons tomato paste

Make Savory Pancake Filling (see below). Keep warm. Sift flour into a medium bowl. Gradually stir in ¼ cup of water. Beat mixture well, breaking up any lumps. Add remaining water, turmeric, salt and red pepper; beat mixture again.

Heat oil in a small, heavy, nonstick skillet over medium heat. When oil is hot, add mixture and spread it over bottom of skillet. Shake gently to prevent sticking. After 3 or 4 minutes, when the first side is crisp and light brown, turn the pancake. Cook other side. Place on a warm plate. Pour Savory Pancake Filling on pancake. Makes 1 serving.

Savory Pancake Filling:
Heat oil in a small skillet over medium heat. Add apple, celery and bell pepper. Sauté until they are soft, stirring often. Add mung beans, tomato and tomato paste. Mix well. Add a little water if necessary to prevent sticking. Cook mixture for 5 minutes. Serve warm. Makes 1 serving.

Oriental Vegetables ★ W M E A

1 garlic clove, cut in half
1 tablespoon soy oil
2 medium carrots, sliced into
strips

¼ lb. okra
¼ lb. button mushrooms, sliced
¾ lb. bean sprouts
Salt and pepper to taste

Rub cut garlic clove inside a nonstick skillet. Heat 2 teaspoons of oil in skillet over medium-low heat. Add carrots. Cover and sauté carrots until slightly tender. While carrots are cooking, cut stems of okra close to the pod, but do not cut into pod. Add trimmed okra to carrots; cover pan. Cook 5 to 7 minutes. Add mushrooms, bean sprouts, salt, pepper and the remaining teaspoon of oil to mixture. Stir well. Increase heat to medium high; cover pan. Sauté mixture, stirring occasionally, 10 minutes. Makes 2 servings.

Garbanzo Beans & Tomatoes   ★ Ⓜ Ⓜ Ⓔ

½ cup garbanzo beans
2 tablespoons sunflower oil
1 small green bell pepper
1 garlic clove, crushed

8 tomatoes, chopped
2 pinches of dried leaf parsley
2 pinches of dried leaf thyme
Salt and pepper to taste

Place beans in a medium saucepan with enough water to cover by 2 inches. Soak overnight. Drain; set aside. Heat oil in a medium saucepan. Add bell pepper and garlic; fry until bell pepper is soft. Add tomatoes, drained beans, parsley, thyme, salt and pepper. Mix well. Add a little water if mixture begins drying out. Cover pan with tight-fitting lid. Simmer until beans are tender, about 45 minutes. Makes 2 servings.

Cheese Fruit & Nut Loaf   Ⓜ Ⓜ Ⓔ

See photograph, page 70

6 oz. shredded goat's milk
   Cheddar cheese (1½ cups)
3 oz. feta cheese
Soy milk
1 large dried apricot, chopped

1 tablespoon chopped
   hazelnuts
1 tablespoon golden raisins
1 large prune, chopped
Chopped nuts

In a medium bowl, combine Cheddar cheese and feta cheese. Add enough soy milk to moisten and bind. Place ½ of the cheese mixture on a large foil sheet in a rectangle about 7" x 2". Sprinkle apricot, hazelnuts, golden raisins and prune on top. Cover with remaining cheese mixture. Wrap tightly. Refrigerate overnight. Unwrap; decorate with chopped nuts. Makes 6 to 8 servings.

Fruit & Nut Snack   𝕎   𝕄   𝔼

See photograph, page 70

¾ cup unsalted peanuts
1¼ cups chopped dried apricots
1¼ cups golden raisins

½ cup sunflower seeds
½ cup chopped walnuts

Place ingredients in a large bowl. Mix well; store in an airtight container. Makes about 4 cups.

Fish

Trout with Cucumber ★ 𝖂 𝖬 𝖤 𝖠

1 cucumber, peeled and coarsely chopped	¼ cup millet flour, seasoned with salt and pepper
4 trout, cleaned	6 tablespoons kosher margarine
	Freshly ground pepper

In a medium saucepan, combine cucumber and a little salted water. Bring to a boil. Cook 3 to 4 minutes. Drain cucumber; pat dry with paper towels.

Roll trout in seasoned flour. Melt margarine in a large skillet. Add floured trout; cook, turning once, until trout turns from transparent to opaque, 15 to 20 minutes. Remove trout from skillet; drain on paper towels. Keep warm. Add cucumber to skillet in which trout were cooked. Cook gently 5 minutes. Add salt and pepper.

Place trout on a serving dish. Arrange cucumber around trout; serve immediately. Makes 4 servings.

Baked Stuffed Trout 𝖂 𝖬 𝖤

4 trout, cleaned	⅓ cup chopped walnuts
1 Granny Smith apple, peeled and chopped	1 tablespoon water
2 celery stalks, sliced	3 tablespoons kosher margarine
	Salt and pepper to taste

Preheat oven to 350F (175C).

Rinse trout and pat dry with paper towels. Place apple, celery, walnuts and water in a medium saucepan. Cover and simmer until apple softens. Stir well.

Grease a large shallow baking dish with a little margarine. Pack ¼ of apple mixture into each trout. Arrange stuffed trout in greased dish. Add salt and pepper; dot the fish with remaining margarine. Bake in preheated oven until fish turns from transparent to opaque, about 20 minutes, basting frequently. Serve hot. Makes 4 servings.

Fish Cakes (*above*, see page 73); Baked Stuffed Trout (*below*)

Italian Halibut

4 (1-inch-thick) halibut steaks
1 tablespoon olive oil
1 celery stalk, chopped
1 red bell pepper, chopped
1 lb. tomatoes, peeled and
  seeded

1 teaspoon dried leaf basil
Salt and pepper to taste
2 tablespoons chopped parsley

Preheat oven to 400F (205C).
  Grease a baking dish large enough to hold fish in a single layer.
Place fish in greased dish. Heat olive oil in a large skillet over
medium heat. Add celery and bell pepper; sauté until wilted. Add
tomatoes, basil, salt and pepper; simmer 10 minutes. Pour tomato
mixture over fish. Cover the dish.
  Bake in preheated oven 15 minutes. Remove cover; bake until
fish turns from transparent to opaque, about 7 minutes. Garnish
with parsley. Makes 4 servings.

Fish with Sorrel Sauce ⭐ Ⓦ Ⓜ Ⓔ Ⓐ

4 portions of cod, haddock or
  flounder fillets
2 tablespoons kosher margarine

Sorrel Sauce:
2 tablespoons kosher margarine

½ cup sorrel leaves, finely
  chopped
1 rounded tablespoon rice flour
  or millet flour
1¼ cups chicken stock
Salt and pepper to taste

Grease a broiler pan rack. Place oven rack about 6 inches from
heat source. Preheat broiler. Place fish on greased rack; dot with
margarine. Broil until fish turns from transparent to opaque,
about 6 minutes per side. Keep warm. Prepare Sorrel Sauce. Place
fish in a warm serving dish; garnish with parsley. Pour Sorrel Sauce
over fish. Makes 4 servings.

Sorrel Sauce:
Melt margarine in a medium saucepan. Add sorrel; sauté until
sorrel is wilted. Stir in flour. Gradually add chicken stock, stirring
continuously. Stir until sauce has thickened. Add salt and
pepper.

Cheese Fruit & Nut Loaf (*top*, see page 66); Fruit & Nut Snack (*below left*, see page 67); Garbanzo-Bean Pancakes with Savory Pancake Filling (*below right*, see page 65)

Fish Curry   ⊠ Ⓦ Ⓜ Ⓔ

6 to 8 medium tomatoes	1 cup cooked peas or green
1 tablespoon soy oil	beans
4 to 5 teaspoons wheat-free	2 teaspoons cream of coconut
curry powder	(additive free)
⅓ cup red bell pepper, chopped	2 teaspoons Garam Masala, if
2 (4-oz.) frozen cod steaks	desired (see page 30)

Chop tomatoes and save juice. Heat oil in a large skillet. Add curry powder and bell pepper. Sauté 3 minutes; move the pepper to 1 side. Add fish; cook. Fry 4 to 5 minutes on each side, or until thawed. Add tomatoes and juice, and peas or beans. Flake fish into bite-sized pieces. Simmer until fish turns from transparent to opaque, about 5 minutes. Add a little water if mixture begins drying out. Stir in creamed coconut; heat through. Immediately before serving, stir in garam masala, if desired. Makes 2 servings.

Mackerel with Apples   ⊠ Ⓦ Ⓜ Ⓔ Ⓐ

2 small mackerel, cleaned	Salt and pepper to taste
2 small Granny Smith apples,	1 tablespoon kosher margarine
peeled and sliced	⅔ cup unsweetened apple juice

Preheat oven to 350F (175C).

Rinse fish; pat dry with paper towels. Place fish in a shallow baking dish. Add apples. Season with salt and pepper. Dot fish with margarine. Pour apple juice around fish.

Cover dish with foil. Bake in preheated oven until fish turns from transparent to opaque, about 30 minutes. Baste once. Makes 2 servings.

Fish Cakes

W M E A

See photograph, page 69

1 lb. potatoes, sliced
2 cups cooked, flaked white fish
2 tablespoons kosher margarine
2 tablespoons milk substitute

2 tablespoons chopped parsley
Salt and pepper to taste
Millet flakes
Sunflower oil

Boil potatoes in lightly salted water until they are tender, about 10 minutes. Drain. In a medium bowl, combine drained potatoes, fish, margarine and milk substitute. Mash ingredients until well-blended. Add parsley, salt and pepper. Mix well. Put millet flakes on a flat plate. Divide mixture into 10 to 12 equal portions. Using your hands, shape into flat fish cakes. Press millet flakes on fish cakes.

Heat oil in a large skillet. Add fish cakes. Fry until golden brown, about 4 minutes per side. Makes 3 to 4 servings.

Meat

See photograph, page 82

Beef with Vegetables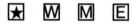

6 to 8 medium tomatoes
2 tablespoons olive oil
10 to 12-oz. beef round steak,
  cut into 1-inch cubes
1 garlic clove, thinly sliced
3 medium carrots, sliced

½ medium green bell pepper,
  chopped
2½ cups cooked red kidney
  beans
Salt and pepper to taste
1 teaspoon chili powder

Chop tomatoes and save juice; set aside. Heat olive oil in a heavy saucepan over medium heat. Add beef; sauté until browned on all sides. Add garlic. Add tomatoes and their juice, carrots, bell pepper and beans to casserole. Stir in salt, pepper and chili powder; mix well. Reduce heat. Cover casserole; simmer until meat is tender, 30 to 40 minutes. Makes 2 servings.

Yorkshire Potted Beef

½ lb. beef for stew, cut into
  ½-inch cubes
Water

½ teaspoon ground mace
Salt and pepper to taste
2 tablespoons kosher margarine

Place beef and enough water to cover in a medium saucepan over low heat. Cover and simmer, stirring frequently, until beef is very tender, about 1½ hours. Drain, reserving broth. Run cooked beef through a meat grinder; repeat. In a medium bowl, combine ground meat, mace, salt, pepper and reserved broth. Spoon into a small mold or bowl. Melt margarine in a small saucepan; pour over meat mixture. Refrigerate until set. Cut into pieces to serve. Makes 2 servings.

Beef & Lentils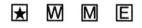

½ cup red lentils
1 lb. beef for stew
1 tablespoon sunflower oil
2½ cups beef stock (see
  page 90)

6 to 8 tomatoes, peeled and
  chopped
1 bay leaf
1 teaspoon dried leaf basil
Salt and pepper to taste

Soak lentils in water overnight. Preheat oven to 350F (175C). Cut meat into cubes. Place oil in medium skillet over medium heat. Add meat; sauté until browned. Transfer meat to a casserole dish. Add lentils, stock, tomatoes, bay leaf, basil, salt and pepper. Cover and bake in preheated oven until meat is tender, about 1½ hours. Makes 4 servings.

Arabian Lamb

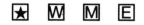

2 tablespoons ground coriander
2 tablespoons ground cumin
1 tablespoon paprika
1 tablespoon brown sugar
1 teaspoon freshly ground pepper
1 large garlic clove, crushed
Pinch of salt
¼ cup olive oil
1 (4- to 4½-lb.) boneless leg of lamb

Begin preparations 4 to 5 hours before roasting the meat. In a medium bowl, combine coriander, cumin, paprika, brown sugar, pepper, garlic, salt and olive oil. Rub mixture all over inside and outside of leg of lamb. Cover and refrigerate at least 4 hours, so flavors soak into meat. Place lamb in roasting pan.

Preheat oven to 425F (220C). Roast 20 minutes per pound, plus an additional 20 minutes, or until lamb is of desired doneness, basting 3 or 4 times. Makes 6 servings.

Stuffed Lamb Shoulder

2 tablespoons olive oil
¼ lb. lamb's liver, diced
1 celery stalk, finely chopped
1 garlic clove, crushed
½ cup cooked rice
⅓ cup dark raisins or golden raisins
1 tablespoon Italian seasoning
1 (3 lb.) boned shoulder of lamb, unrolled
2 rosemary sprigs
Watercress

Preheat oven to 350F (175C).

Heat oil in medium skillet; add liver, celery and garlic. Sauté until liver is no longer pink inside. Combine rice, raisins and Italian seasoning in a large bowl. Add fried ingredients and mix well. Allow to cool.

Stuff lamb with the mixture; secure with skewers or stitching. Place lamb in a roasting dish with rosemary sprigs on top. Roast in preheated oven to desired doneness, 1½ to 2 hours. Drain off fat and place lamb on a serving dish. Garnish with watercress. Makes 6 servings.

Pork Chops with Apples & Ginger

See photograph, page 91

★ Ⓦ Ⓜ Ⓔ

2 tablespoons olive oil
4 pork chops
2 celery stalks, sliced
2 Granny Smith apples, peeled
  and sliced

2 tablespoons granulated sugar
1 (1-inch) piece gingerroot,
  peeled and grated
¾ cup water
2 tablespoons brown sugar

Preheat oven to 350F (175C).
  Heat oil in a large skillet. Add pork chops; sauté until browned on both sides. Place browned chops in a shallow baking dish. Add celery to fat remaining in skillet. Cook until soft. Add apples, granulated sugar and gingerroot. Add water. Bring to a boil. Reduce heat; simmer until apples are soft. Arrange apple mixture on top of pork. Cover with foil. Bake in preheated oven 50 minutes.
  Remove foil, sprinkle with brown sugar. Bake, uncovered, until centers are no longer pink, about 10 minutes. Serve immediately. Makes 4 servings.

Pork & Apple Pie

Ⓦ Ⓜ Ⓔ

1 tablespoon vegetable oil
12 oz. stewing pork, trimmed
  of fat, cubed
1 garlic clove, crushed
1 onion, chopped
1 medium Granny Smith apple,
  peeled, cored, chopped

2 teaspoons golden raisins
Salt and pepper to taste
½ cup apple unsweetened
  juice
1 lb. potatoes, peeled, thinly
  sliced (about 3 cups)
1 tablespoon kosher margarine

Preheat oven to 350F (175C).
  Heat oil in a large skillet. Fry pork, turning frequently, until it is brown on all sides. Transfer pork cubes to an ovenproof dish or casserole. In a bowl, mix together garlic, onion, apple, golden raisins, salt and pepper. Arrange on top of meat. Pour apple juice over meat and vegetables. Arrange potato slices over the top and dot with margarine. Cover with a lid or foil and bake for 1 to 1½ hours. Remove the lid or foil and bake ½ hour to brown the potato topping before serving. Makes 2 servings.

Pork & Bell Pepper Casserole

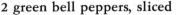

1 lb. lean pork cubes
¼ cup rice flour
Salt and black pepper to taste
2 tablespoons sunflower oil
1 celery stalk, chopped

2 green bell peppers, sliced
2 medium tomatoes, peeled
  and chopped
⅔ cup canned tomato juice
½ teaspoon dried leaf marjoram

Preheat oven to 350F (175C).
Trim any fat off the pork. In a plastic bag, combine flour, salt and black pepper. Add pork; shake to coat pork with seasoned flour. Heat ½ the oil in a large skillet. Add coated pork; sauté until browned, turning frequently. Using a slotted spoon, place meat in a casserole.
Pour remaining oil into skillet. Add celery and green peppers; sauté until soft. Place them in casserole. Add tomatoes, tomato juice and marjoram; mix well. Bake in preheated oven until meat is tender, about 1½ hours. Makes 4 servings.

Marinated Pork

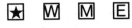

¼ cup olive oil or sunflower
  oil
2 garlic cloves, crushed
1 teaspoon dried leaf thyme

1 rosemary sprig, or 1 teaspoon
  dried rosemary
1 teaspoon chopped parsley
Salt and pepper to taste
⅔ cup unsweetened apple juice
6 pork chops

Combine oil, garlic, thyme, rosemary, parsley, salt and pepper in a plastic bag; add pork. Shake well, then seal the bag. Refrigerate 24 hours. Turn bag 2 or 3 times during this period. Preheat broiler. Remove meat from marinade and place on broiler pan. Broil until centers are no longer pink, about 20 minutes, turning once, and basting frequently with marinade. Makes 6 servings.

Pressed Tongue

1 ox tongue
6 peppercorns
2 celery stalks, chopped

1 carrot, chopped
2 cloves
1 bay leaf

Place tongue in a pressure cooker. Cover with water, gradually bring to a boil, without the lid on, then drain. Lift out trivet, replace tongue, and add the other ingredients. Pour in enough water to come halfway up sides of the pressure cooker. Cook at high pressure for 15 minutes per pound. Remove from heat; allow pressure to subside at room temperature. Lift out tongue and while still warm remove skin and any fat. Curl into a small bowl. Cover with a saucer and add a heavy weight. Retain cooking liquid for use as stock. Allow tongue to cool, then turn out and garnish before serving. Makes 6 servings.

Oriental Stuffed Lamb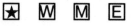

1 (3 lb.) boned shoulder of lamb, unrolled
Salt and pepper to taste
1 tablespoon sunflower oil

Rice & Apricot Stuffing:
2 cups cooked brown rice

¾ cup dried apricots, soaked and chopped
3 tablespoons raisins
⅓ cup pine nuts, lightly roasted
2 garlic cloves, crushed
½ teaspoon ground cinnamon
1 teaspoon ground coriander
1 teaspoon ground ginger
Salt and pepper

Preheat oven to 375F (190C).
Spread out lamb. Season with salt and pepper inside and out. Set aside. Prepare stuffing. Stuff lamb with some of stuffing, secure with skewers or stitching. Place lamb in a roasting pan. Brush lamb with oil; roast 30 minutes per pound, including stuffing, plus an additional 20 minutes.

Place on a serving dish and keep warm. Pour fat away from pan juices; add remaining rice stuffing. Heat on top of stove, adding a little water if necessary. Arrange stuffing around lamb. Makes 4 servings.

Rice & Apricot Stuffing:
In a large bowl, combine rice, apricots, raisins, pine nuts, garlic, cinnamon, coriander, ginger, salt and pepper. Mix well.

Bobotie

3 tablespoons sunflower oil
1½ cups chopped onions
4 garlic cloves, crushed
1½ lbs. ground lamb or beef
1 teaspoon ground turmeric
1 tablespoon wheat-free curry powder
2 tablespoons white-wine vinegar
⅔ cup beef stock
2 tomatoes, peeled and chopped

2 tablespoons blanched almonds, chopped
⅓ cup golden raisins
⅓ cup dried apricots, soaked and chopped
1 tablespoon brown sugar
1 banana, chopped
2 eggs
1¼ cups milk substitute
Thin slices of lemon
3 to 4 fresh bay leaves

Oriental Stuffed Lamb (*above*); Bobotie (*below*)
OVERLEAF: Chicken with Fruit (*top left and right*, see page 85); Prune-Striped Turkey (*below left*, see page 88)

Preheat oven to 350F (175C).
Heat oil in a skillet over medium heat. Add onions and garlic;
cook until lightly browned. Add lamb or beef. Cook until meat is
browned. Drain off fat. Add turmeric, curry powder, vinegar,
stock and tomatoes. Cook uncovered for 10 minutes. Add
almonds, golden raisins, apricots, sugar and banana. Mix well.
Spoon the mixture into a shallow casserole dish.
Place eggs and milk substitute in a medium bowl. Beat until
combined. Pour custard mixture over top of meat mixture.
Arrange lemon slices and bay leaves in custard. Bake in preheated
oven until custard is set, about 30 minutes. Makes 6 servings.

Variation:
If eggs cannot be tolerated, omit custard topping.

Deviled Kidneys ★ W M E

1 tablespoon wheat-free
  mustard powder
1 teaspoon wheat-free curry
  powder
1 tablespoon rice flour

4 lamb's kidneys, skinned,
  cored and cut in half
4 tablespoons kosher margarine
2 tablespoons tomato paste
1¼ cups water
Salt and pepper to taste

In a shallow bowl, combine mustard powder, curry powder and
rice flour. Coat kidneys with this mixture. Melt margarine in a
large skillet. Add the kidneys; sauté about 5 minutes, turning
frequently, until they are lightly browned. Stir in tomato paste,
water, salt and pepper. Bring to a boil. Reduce heat; cover.
Simmer 20 minutes or until kidneys are tender. Makes 2
servings.

Beef with Vegetables (see page 74)

Corsican Liver   ⊠ ☒ ☒ ☒

2 tablespoons olive oil
1 garlic clove, crushed
1 green bell pepper, chopped
1 lb. pork or lamb's liver, sliced
1 lb. tomatoes, peeled and
   seeded
1 tablespoon brown-rice miso

1¼ cups hot water
1 teaspoon dried leaf basil
½ teaspoon dried rosemary
½ teaspoon dried leaf thyme
½ lb. green beans, cut into
   2-inch pieces
2 tablespoons chopped parsley

Preheat oven to 400F (205C).
Heat oil in a large skillet over medium heat. Add garlic and bell pepper; sauté until soft. Using a slotted spoon, place in a shallow baking dish. Place liver in skillet; sauté 2 to 3 minutes on each side. Remove with slotted spoon and place on top of garlic and bell pepper.
Place tomatoes in skillet. In a small bowl, dissolve miso in hot water and pour into skillet. Add basil, rosemary and thyme. Simmer 3 to 4 minutes, stirring continuously. Add beans to mixture; bring to a boil. Pour mixture over liver. Cover and bake in preheated oven until beans are tender, about 30 minutes. Makes 4 servings.

Poultry

Stuffing for Roast Chicken ☒ ☒ ☒ ☒

2 tablespoons sunflower oil
1 celery stalk, finely chopped
2 garlic cloves, crushed
⅓ cup uncooked long-grain
   white rice
⅔ cup hot water

¼ lb. mushrooms, sliced
2 tablespoons golden raisins
2 oz. dried apricots (½ cup),
   soaked and chopped
2 teaspoons dried leaf tarragon
Salt and pepper to taste

Heat oil in large skillet. Add celery and garlic; sauté over medium heat 2 to 3 minutes. Add rice; sauté 3 minutes, stirring. Pour in hot water. Stir, then simmer 10 minutes or until most of the water has been absorbed but rice is still slightly hard. Remove from heat; mix in remaining ingredients.
Allow to cool to room temperature before using. Makes about 3 cups.

Chicken with Fruit

See photograph, page 80

6 oz. dried apricots (about 1¼ cups) or 4 bananas

4 whole chicken breasts, boned and skinned
1 cup shredded coconut
6 tablespoons kosher margarine

Soak apricots overnight in a medium saucepan with enough water to cover. Simmer until tender and water is absorbed, about 10 minutes. Or, slice bananas in half lengthwise.

Stuff chicken breasts with apricots or 2 banana halves. Secure with wooden picks. Pour coconut on cutting board or counter. Roll each chicken breast in the coconut.

Melt margarine in large skillet. Add chicken breasts; sauté over medium heat 2 minutes on each side. Remove from skillet; roll in coconut again. Return to skillet; reduce heat. Cook 8 to 10 minutes or until juices run clear when chicken is pierced. Serve immediately. Makes 4 servings.

Oriental Chicken

6 tablespoons kosher margarine
2 tablespoons olive oil
1 lb. chicken breasts, cut into strips about 2 inches long and ½ inch wide
1 (1-inch) piece gingerroot, grated
2 celery stalks, finely chopped
1 green bell pepper, cut into strips

8 carrots, cut into strips
¼ lb. button mushrooms, sliced
2 large tomatoes, peeled, seeded and sliced
3¾ cups bean sprouts
½ teaspoon Italian seasoning
Salt and black pepper to taste
2 tablespoons wheat-free tamari sauce

Heat margarine and oil in a large skillet or wok. Add chicken and gingerroot. Stir-fry over medium heat 3 to 4 minutes. Add celery, bell pepper and carrots. Stir-fry 4 minutes. Add mushrooms and tomatoes. Stir-fry 3 minutes, adding the bean sprouts after 2 minutes. Add Italian seasoning, salt, black pepper and tamari sauce. Stir-fry 1 minute. Makes 4 servings.

Spicy Chicken

4 chicken legs or thighs,
  skinned
2 tablespoons chopped parsley
5 tablespoons kosher margarine
½ cup honey
Salt and pepper to taste

1 teaspoon wheat-free curry
  powder
⅛ teaspoon each of: ground
  cumin, chili powder, ground
  coriander, ground cinnamon,
  ground ginger, ground
  nutmeg and ground cloves
Additional chopped parsley

Preheat oven to 350F (175C).
   Place chicken in a shallow baking dish. Sprinkle 2 tablespoons parsley over chicken. Melt margarine in a pan; add honey, salt and spices. Mix well. Pour over chicken. Cover with foil. Bake in preheated oven until chicken is tender, about 1 hour, removing foil for last 15 minutes. Garnish with parsley. Makes 4 servings.

Chicken in a Coconut

4 coconuts
2 red bell peppers, seeded and
  chopped
2 green bell peppers, seeded
  and chopped

¼ lb. mushrooms, sliced
1 celery stalk, finely chopped
Salt and pepper to taste
3 cups diced, cooked chicken
About 2 cups millet flour

Preheat oven to 325F (165C).
   Wash coconuts. Saw off tops and pour coconut milk into a pitcher. Place bell peppers, mushrooms and celery in a medium saucepan; add coconut milk, salt and pepper. Gradually bring mixture to a boil. Reduce heat; simmer until bell peppers are soft. Stir in chicken. Reheat, adding a little water if necessary.
   Fill coconuts with chicken mixture. Replace lids. In a small bowl, make a paste of millet flour and enough water to make a thick paste. Seal lids with paste. Bake in preheated oven 1½ hours. Makes 4 servings.

Spicy Chicken Salad

1¼ cups soy milk
¼ cup water
3 garlic cloves, crushed
1¼ cups shredded coconut
1 teaspoon cilantro
½ teaspoon ground cumin
⅔ cup goat's milk yogurt

Salt and pepper to taste
3 cups diced, cooked chicken
   or turkey
1 lb. tomatoes, peeled, seeded
   and sliced
Chopped fresh parsley
Paprika

Place milk in a medium saucepan. Add water, garlic, coconut, cilantro and cumin. Bring to a boil. Reduce heat; simmer 2 to 3 minutes. Allow to cool. Drain through a cheesecloth or fine sieve. Press down hard to extract all liquid. In a small bowl, mix liquid with yogurt. Add salt and pepper.
   Place chicken or turkey in a serving dish. Add tomatoes. Pour yogurt mixture over chicken and tomatoes. Cover and refrigerate until chilled. Garnish with parsley and paprika. Makes 4 servings.

Chicken & Rice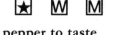

¾ cup uncooked brown rice
2 cups water, very hot but not
   boiling
1 tablespoon brown-rice miso
2 teaspoons tomato paste

Salt and pepper to taste
4 chicken legs
1 bouquet garni
Parsley sprigs

Place rice in a heavy medium saucepan with a tight-fitting lid. Add hot water; stir in miso, tomato paste, salt and pepper. Cover; bring to a boil. Remove cover; stir well. Add chicken legs and bouquet garni. Replace lid; simmer 35 to 40 minutes, until rice has absorbed all water. Check occasionally to make sure mixture is not drying out; add water if necessary. Garnish with parsley. Makes 2 servings.

Chicken in Mango Sauce

4 boneless chicken breast
   halves, skinned
1 mango

Pinch of salt
2 tablespoons water
1 tablespoon mango chutney

Preheat broiler. Grease a broiler-pan rack. Place chicken on broiler-pan rack. Broil 25 minutes; turn chicken. Broil about 10 minutes or until juices run clear when chicken is pierced.

→

Halve the mango; scoop out flesh, discarding the skin. Place mango in a medium saucepan with salt and water. Cook over low heat until mango is soft enough to mash. Consistency of mashed mango should be a bit firmer than applesauce. Stir in mango chutney.

Place broiled chicken in a serving dish. Pour hot mango sauce on top. Serve immediately. Makes 4 servings.

Crispy Chicken with Herbed Tomatoes   ★ Ⓦ Ⓜ Ⓔ

2 boneless chicken breast
  halves, skinned
2 tablespoons kosher
  margarine, room temperature
Salt and pepper to taste

2 tomatoes
1 teaspoon sugar
4 pinches of Italian seasoning
Watercress

Preheat broiler. Grease a small broiler-pan rack. Place chicken breasts on broiler-pan rack. Broil until browned, about 15 minutes. Lift out broiler pan; turn over chicken. Spread margarine evenly over each piece; sprinkle with salt and pepper. Halve tomatoes; sprinkle salt, pepper, sugar and Italian seasoning onto cut surfaces. Place on broiler pan around chicken. Broil until chicken is cooked and tomatoes are soft, about 5 minutes. Garnish with watercress. Makes 2 servings.

See photograph, page 80

Prune-Striped Turkey   ★ Ⓦ Ⓜ Ⓔ Ⓐ

4 to 5 prunes
Water
2 turkey-breast fillets
Salt and pepper to taste

Pat of kosher margarine, if
  desired
Salt and pepper to taste
Chopped parsley to garnish

Place prunes in a small saucepan. Add enough water to barely cover. Simmer about 5 minutes, until prunes are soft. Remove from heat. Pit and mash prunes. Set aside.

Preheat broiler. Grease a broiler-pan rack. Place turkey breasts on broiler-pan rack. Season with salt and pepper; dot with margarine. Broil 10 minutes; turn turkey. Make a cut into, but not all the way through, the uncooked side of turkey breasts. Pack prune puree into each slit. Broil 5 to 10 minutes, or until turkey juices run clear when turkey is pierced. Garnish with parsley and serve. Makes 2 servings.

Duck with Olives

1 (4-lb.) duck, ready to cook
Salt
2 garlic cloves, crushed
2 cups red bell pepper, chopped
¼ lb. button mushrooms

4 medium tomatoes, peeled, seeded and chopped
Salt and pepper to taste
¼ cup pimento-stuffed green olives

Preheat oven to 350F (175C).
Prick duck skin all over; rub with salt. Put duck in a roasting pan. Roast in preheated oven until juices run clear when duck is pierced, about 2 hours. Remove from pan; discard most of fat. Keep duck warm.
Place roasting pan over medium heat. Add garlic and bell pepper. Sauté until soft. Add mushrooms and tomatoes; cook over low heat 7 minutes. Add salt and pepper.
Divide duck into 4 portions. Place in a small baking dish. Pour bell pepper mixture on top. Cover and bake 45 minutes. Add olives 10 minutes before end of cooking time. Makes 4 servings.

Marinated Duck

2 duck quarters
1 (1-inch) piece gingerroot, grated
2 tablespoons olive oil
2 tablespoons honey

2 tablespoons unsweetened apple juice
1 tablespoon wheat-free tamari sauce
Watercress

Slash duck skin in 3 or 4 places.
Mix gingerroot, olive oil, honey, apple juice and tamari sauce in medium bowl. Pour over duck. Marinate in the refrigerator at least 4 hours, turning frequently.
Preheat broiler. Grease a broiler-pan rack. Drain duck; dry with paper towels. Broil duck 25 minutes, turning once and basting with marinade 4 or 5 times. Juices should run clear when duck is pierced. Garnish with watercress. Makes 2 servings.

Variation:
•You can also put duck in a roasting pan and bake 40 minutes at 400F (205C). Baste duck several times.

Stocks, Sauces & Jams

Vegetable Stock

Vegetable leftovers and parts,
  such as outer leaves of
  cabbage and spinach
½ teaspoon salt

Wash and store vegetable leftovers and parts in a plastic bag in the refrigerator. When you are ready to make stock, chop vegetables; place them in a large saucepan. Cover with water. Bring to a boil over high heat. Boil 15 minutes. Remove from heat. Drain off liquid; cool quickly. Refrigerate up to 2 days or freeze up to 3 months.

Tip

The water in which vegetables are cooked is an economical and healthful substitute for stock.

Meat or Chicken Stock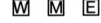

Meat or poultry bones

Place bones in a large saucepan. Cover with water. Bring to a boil over high heat. Reduce heat; simmer 3 hours, skimming grey foam from surface. Remove from heat. Drain off liquid; refrigerate until chilled. Lift off fat from top of stock. Refrigerate up to 2 days or freeze up to 2 months.

Variation:
You can also prepare stock by placing bones and water in a pressure cooker and cooking 30 minutes.

Purees

You can use vegetable purees to replace gravy mixes and bouillon cubes. You can make purees in great quantities and freeze them for later use.

Pork Chops with Apples & Ginger (see page 76)

Egg-Free Mayonnaise

½ teaspoon sea salt
1 teaspoon sugar
1 teaspoon wheat-free dry
  mustard
Pepper

1 tablespoon rice flour
1 teaspoon arrowroot
4 tablespoon olive oil
4 tablespoons vinegar
1 cup milk substitute

Place salt, sugar, mustard, pepper, flour and arrowroot in a medium saucepan. Mix well. Stir in oil. Gradually add vinegar. Stir in milk substitute. Bring to a boil over medium-low heat, stirring continuously. Cook until sauce has thickened. Allow to cool. Adjust seasoning if necessary. Makes 1 cup.

Green Bell Pepper Sauce ★ W M E A

3 cups green bell pepper,
  chopped
4 garlic cloves
7 tablespoons safflower oil

1 tablespoon unsweetened
  apple juice
Salt and black pepper to taste

Place bell pepper and garlic in a medium saucepan. Cover with water; bring to a boil. Reduce heat; simmer 10 minutes. Drain off water. Place garlic and bell pepper in a blender or food processor fitted with a steel blade. Process until pureed. With motor running, slowly add oil. Add apple juice, salt and black pepper. Process until combined. Pour sauce back into saucepan and slowly warm over low heat. Makes about 2 cups.

Tip

You can make this sauce into a salad dressing by adding ½ cup chopped cucumber and 2 tablespoons goat's milk yogurt to the mixture when you process it in the blender or food processor.

Walnut Raita

2½ cups goat's milk or sheep's
  milk yogurt
⅓ cup chopped walnuts

2 tablespoons cilantro, finely
  chopped
1 small onion, finely chopped
Salt and pepper to taste

In a medium bowl, beat yogurt until smooth and creamy. Add remaining ingredients; mix well. Makes 4 servings.

From the top: Tofu Spread (see page 63); Deep-Fried Mung Beans (see page 64); Cucumber Dip (see page 63); Bean & Apple Dip (see page 64)

Coconut Sauce ★ Ⓦ Ⓜ Ⓔ Ⓐ

½ cup cream of coconut
  (additive-free)
⅔ cup hot water

Combine cream of coconut with hot water in a small bowl. Beat mixture until smooth. Makes 2 servings.

Black-Currant Jam ★ Ⓦ Ⓜ Ⓔ

1½ lbs. fresh black currants,   5 cups water
  trimmed   3½ lbs. sugar

Place currants and water in a large pan. Boil 30 minutes. Add sugar; boil rapidly until jam begins to thicken, about 15 minutes. Pour into warm dry jars and seal according to manufacturer's instructions. Makes 7 to 8 pints.

Tip

To test jams for doneness, chill a small plate. Remove jam from heat. Place a spoonful of hot mixture on plate. Place in freezer 1 minute. After 1 minute there should not be watery liquid around edge. Draw your finger through mixture; trough should remain.

Raspberry or Loganberry Jam ★ Ⓦ Ⓜ Ⓔ

2 lbs. raspberries or   ½ tablespoon water
  loganberries   1¾ lbs. sugar

Place raspberries (or loganberries) and water in a large pan. Cook over low heat until berries are soft. Add sugar; bring to a boil quickly. Boil rapidly until jam begins to thicken, about 15 minutes. Pour into warm, dry jars and seal according to manufacturer's instructions. Makes 4 to 6 pints.

Tip

To test jams for doneness, chill a small plate. Remove jam from heat. Place a spoonful of hot mixture on plate. Place in freezer 1 minute. After 1 minute, there should be no watery liquid around edge. Draw your finger through mixture; trough should remain.

Blackberry & Apple Jelly

3 lbs. blackberries
¾ cup water

5 medium green apples,
quartered
12 oz. sugar for each
4 cups juice

Place blackberries and water in a large saucepan. Bring to a boil. Reduce heat; simmer until berries are soft and water is dark red. Drain through a jelly bag or cheesecloth-lined sieve. Allow berries to drain overnight to obtain as much juice as possible. Save juice. Place apples in a medium saucepan and cover with cold water. Bring to a boil. Reduce heat; simmer until apples are very soft. Drain the same way as the berries. Allow apples to drain overnight. Save juice.

Mix and measure juices. Pour into a large pan. Add sugar. Boil about 20 minutes, until mixture reaches setting point, 220F (105C). Pour into warm, dry jars and seal according to manufacturer's instructions. Makes about 5 pints.

Plum Jam ★ W M E

6 lbs. plums, pitted
3¾ cups water
6 lbs. sugar

Place plums in a large pan. Add water; simmer until plums are soft. Add sugar; boil rapidly until mixture reaches setting point, 220F (105C). Pour into warm, dry jars and seal according to manufacturer's instructions. Makes about 10 pints.

Tip

To test jams for doneness, chill a small plate. Remove jam from heat. Place a spoonful of hot mixture on plate. Place in freezer 1 minute. After 1 minute, there should be no watery liquid around edge. Draw your finger through mixture; trough should remain.

Bread & Pastry

Baking powder contains starch such as rice flour, cornstarch and commercial wheat flour. Always check the list of ingredients on baking powder to make sure it is safe for you. If you are unable to find a suitable baking powder you can make your own.

The recipes in this book are made with commercial wheat-free baking powder. If using homemade, slightly more is required. For example, if 2 teaspoons baking powder are needed for a recipe, use 3 teaspoons homemade powder.

Homemade Wheat-Free Baking Powder

¼ cup rice flour
¼ cup bicarbonate of soda
¼ cup cream of tartar

Sift together ingredients at least 3 times into a large bowl. Store in an airtight container in a dry place.

Coconut Loaf

Ⓜ Ⓜ

½ cup kosher margarine
½ cup sugar
2 eggs
1¼ cups rice flour

1½ teaspoons wheat-free baking powder (see above)
3 tablespoons shredded coconut
2 tablespoons soy milk
Powdered sugar

Preheat oven to 350F (175C). Grease a 9" x 5" loaf pan with kosher margarine. Place margarine and sugar in a medium bowl; cream until light and fluffy. Beat in eggs, 1 at a time.

Sift rice flour and baking powder twice into a medium bowl. Fold half the flour into the margarine, sugar and egg mixture. Fold in the remaining flour. Stir in coconut and the soy milk until combined.

Pour batter into greased pan. Bake in preheated oven until a wooden pick inserted into center comes out clean, about 1¼ hours. Remove from pan. Place on wire rack to cool. Dust with powdered sugar. Makes 1 loaf.

Simple Banana Loaf

1½ cups millet flour
2 teaspoons wheat-free baking
  powder (see page 96)
½ teaspoon baking soda

5 tablespoons kosher margarine
⅔ cup sugar
2 eggs
4 ripe bananas, mashed

Preheat oven to 375F (190C). Grease a 9" x 5" loaf pan with kosher margarine.

Sift millet flour, baking powder and baking soda into a medium bowl. In another medium bowl, cream margarine and sugar until light and fluffy. Beat in eggs, 1 at a time. Add dry ingredients to creamed mixture alternately with bananas.

Pour batter into greased pan. Bake in preheated oven until a wooden pick inserted into center comes out clean, about 1 hour. Let cool in pan 10 minutes. Remove from pan. Place on wire rack to cool. Makes 1 loaf.

Banana Bread

1½ cups rice flour
2 teaspoons wheat-free baking
  powder (see page 96)
½ teaspoon salt

½ cup kosher margarine, cut
  into pieces
1 lb. ripe bananas, mashed
2 eggs
¾ cup sugar
½ cup chopped walnuts

Preheat oven to 350F (175C). Grease a 9" x 5" loaf pan with kosher margarine.

Sift flour, baking powder and salt in a medium bowl. Cut margarine into flour mixture. Place bananas in another medium bowl; beat eggs into bananas. Add flour and margarine mixture; mix well. Pour into greased pan.

Bake in preheated oven until a wooden pick inserted into center comes out clean, about 1 hour. Let cool in pan 10 minutes. Remove from pan. Place on wire rack to cool. Makes 1 loaf.

Tip

Adding candied peel and the grated peel of ½ an orange makes the bread more moist.

See photograph, page 102

Date & Walnut Loaf

1 cup dates, pitted and firmly packed down	1 teaspoon wheat-free baking powder (see page 96)
1 teaspoon baking soda	½ cup kosher margarine
Pinch of salt	½ cup chopped walnuts
1¼ cups hot water	½ cup brown sugar, packed
2 cups rice flour	1 egg, beaten

Preheat oven to 350F (175C). Grease a 9" x 5" loaf pan with kosher margarine.

Place dates, baking soda and salt in a medium bowl; pour hot water over the top. Allow to cool.

Sift flour and baking powder together twice into a medium bowl. Cut margarine into flour. Drain dates; mix them into flour. Mix walnuts and sugar into flour. Beat in egg. Pour batter into greased pan.

Bake in preheated oven until a wooden pick inserted into center comes out clean, about 1 hour. Let cool in pan 10 minutes. Remove from pan. Place on wire rack to cool. Makes 1 loaf.

Variation:
Substitute currants or raisins for dates.

Apple & Walnut Loaf

½ cup kosher margarine	Pinch of salt
⅔ cup sugar	1 teaspoon pumpkin-pie spice
2 eggs, beaten	1 Granny Smith apple, peeled, cored and chopped
1½ cups millet flour	⅔ cup chopped walnuts
3 teaspoons wheat-free baking powder (see page 96)	

Preheat oven to 350F (175C). Grease a 9" x 5" loaf pan with kosher margarine.

Place margarine and sugar in a large bowl; cream until light and fluffy. Add eggs; mix well. Sift flour, baking powder, salt and pumpkin-pie spice twice; stir into batter. Add apple and walnuts. Mix well. Pour batter into greased pan.

Bake in preheated oven until wooden pick inserted into center comes out clean, about 1 hour. Let cool in pan 10 minutes. Remove from pan. Place on wire rack to cool. Makes 1 loaf.

See photograph, page 102

Yogurt & Raisin Scones

1¾ cups millet flour	⅓ cup raisins
¼ cup sugar	⅔ cup goat's milk yogurt
4 teaspoons wheat-free baking	Soy milk
powder (see page 96)	2 tablespoons brown sugar
3 tablespoons kosher margarine	

Preheat oven to 425F (220C). Grease a baking sheet with kosher margarine.

Sift flour, sugar and baking powder into a medium bowl. Cut in margarine. Add golden raisins. Stir in yogurt; stir until dough forms a ball.

Dust a pastry board and rolling pin with millet flour. Roll out batter to a thickness of about ¾ inch. Cut into rounds with a 1¼-inch cookie cutter. Brush rounds with soy milk; place on greased baking sheet. Sprinkle scones with brown sugar. Bake in preheated oven until browned, 7 minutes. Makes 16 scones.

Sweet Pastry   Ⓜ Ⓜ

⅓ cup ground almonds	Pinch of salt
¼ cup rice flour	3 tablespoons kosher margarine
3 tablespoons sugar	2 egg yolks

In a medium bowl, combine almonds, flour, sugar and salt. Make a well in center. Add margarine and egg yolks to well. Using your fingers, work margarine and egg yolks into flour mixture. Work into a firm dough; add a little water to bind, if necessary. Wrap in plastic wrap and refrigerate 20 minutes. Dust a pastry board and rolling pin with millet flour. Preheat oven to 375F (190C). Grease an 8-inch pie pan. Roll out dough on floured surface to a 9-inch circle. Line pan with dough. Prick dough with a fork. Bake in preheated oven until browned, 10 to 12 minutes. Makes 1 (8-inch) pastry shell.

Cakes & Cookies

Eggless Fruit Cake ★ Ⓦ Ⓜ Ⓔ

2 cups water
⅔ cup currants
⅔ cup raisins
1 cup kosher margarine
¾ cup light brown sugar
1 scant cup millet flour

1 scant cup rice flour
1 tablespoon wheat-free
  baking powder (see page 96)
1 teaspoon baking soda
1 teaspoon pumpkin-pie spice

Preheat oven to 375 F (190 C). Grease a round 8-inch baking pan with kosher margarine.

Place water, currants, raisins, margarine and sugar in a medium saucepan. Bring to a boil. Reduce heat; simmer 5 minutes. Let cool.

Sift together millet flour, rice flour, baking powder, baking soda and pumpkin-pie spice 3 times into a medium bowl. Pour into cooled fruit mixture. Mix until thoroughly blended.

Spoon batter into greased pan. Bake in preheated oven until a wooden pick inserted into center comes out clean, about 50 minutes. Let cool in pan 10 minutes. Remove from pan. Place on wire rack to cool. Makes 1 cake.

Coconut & Raspberry Jelly Roll Ⓦ Ⓜ

2 large eggs
1 cup sugar
1 cup millet flour
½ cup shredded coconut

¾ cup Raspberry Jam
  (see page 94)
Powdered sugar

Preheat oven to 400 F (205 C). Line and grease an 11″ × 7″ jelly-roll pan with kosher margarine.

Put eggs and sugar in a small bowl. Whisk over a pan of hot water until thick and creamy. Remove from heat; whisk until cold.

Sift flour through a fine sieve 3 times. Fold sifted flour into egg ➡

Coconut & Raspberry Jelly Roll (*left*); Honey Cake (*right*, see page 105); Ginger Cookies (*center*, see page 109)
OVERLEAF LEFT: Date & Walnut Loaf (*left*, see page 98); Yogurt & Raisin Scones (*below*, see page 99)
OVERLEAF RIGHT: Black Currant & Tofu Whip (*top*, see page 116); Millet & Hazelnut Ice Cream (*center*, see page 117); Carob Ice Cream (*below*, see page 116)

mixture using a metal spoon. Then fold in 3 tablespoons of coconut in the same way.

Pour batter into greased pan. Bake 12 minutes, or until top is light brown and springs back when gently pushed with a finger.

Turn jelly roll onto waxed paper. Warm jam in a small saucepan. Spread jam on top of jelly roll. Roll up, using waxed paper to help. Dust with powdered sugar and remaining coconut. Makes 1 jelly roll.

Rice Sponge Cake

½ cup kosher margarine, room
  temperature
½ cup sugar
2 eggs
Vanilla extract to taste

1 cup ground rice
1 rounded teaspoon wheat-free
  baking powder (see page 96)
Pinch of salt
Water

Preheat oven to 350F (175C). Grease a round 8-inch baking pan with kosher margarine.

Cream margarine and sugar in a medium bowl; beat in eggs and vanilla extract. Sift ground rice, baking powder and salt into a medium bowl. Add egg, sugar and margarine mixture. Mix well. Add a little water to obtain a firm but soft consistency; too much will cause rice to sink in the cake during baking.

Spoon batter into greased pan. Bake until golden brown, 30 to 40 minutes. Do not open oven door during baking. Let cool in pan several minutes. Remove from pan. Place on wire rack to cool. Makes 1 cake.

See photograph, page 101

Honey Cake ★ Ⓜ Ⓜ Ⓔ

1⅓ cups honey
1⅓ cups soybean oil
1 (¼-oz.) envelope gelatin,
  dissolved in 1⅓ cups hot
  water and cooled to room
  temperature
3 cups buckwheat flour

5 teaspoons wheat-free baking
  powder (see page 96)

Filling:
½ cup kosher margarine
⅓ cup powdered sugar
Soy milk

Preheat oven to 350F (175C). Grease 2 round 8-inch baking pans with kosher margarine and line base and sides with foil.

In a medium bowl, beat together honey, oil and gelatin mixture. Stir together flour and baking powder in a small bowl.

➡

Poached Peaches with Raspberry Sauce (*left*, see page 112); Glazed Pears with Golden Raisins (*right*, see page 114)

Beat into honey mixture. Pour batter into greased pans. Bake 40 to 45 minutes. Let cool in pans several minutes. Remove from pans. Place on wire rack to cool.

Prepare filling. Spread half on 1 layer. Place second layer firmly on top. Cover with the remaining filling. Decorate with seasonal fresh fruit. Makes 1 two-layer cake.

Filling:
In a medium bowl, beat margarine, sugar and a little soy milk until smooth and creamy.

Banana Cake

1 cup plus 2 tablespoons ground rice	½ cup dark brown sugar, packed
1 tablespoon wheat-free baking powder (see page 96)	¼ cup kosher margarine, room temperature
2 pinches of salt	⅔ cup golden raisins and currants, mixed
1 teaspoon ground cinnamon	1 large banana, mashed
	2 eggs

Preheat oven to 375 F (190C). Grease a round 8-inch baking pan with kosher margarine.

Sift together rice, baking powder, salt and cinnamon into a medium bowl. Add sugar. Mix well. Chop margarine into pieces. Add margarine, golden raisins, currants and banana; mix well. Add egg. Beat batter until smooth and well-blended.

Pour batter into greased pan. Bake 35 to 40 minutes. Let cool in pan several minutes. Remove from pan. Place on wire rack to cool. Makes 1 cake.

Eggless Banana Cake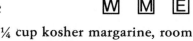

1 cup plus 2 tablespoons ground rice	¼ cup kosher margarine, room temperature
1 tablespoon wheat-free baking powder (see page 96)	⅔ cup golden raisins and currants, mixed
2 pinches of salt	1 large banana, mashed
1 teaspoon ground cinnamon	1 (¼-oz.) envelope unflavored gelatin, dissolved in ⅓ cup hot water and cooled to room temperature
½ cup dark brown sugar, packed	

Preheat oven to 375 F (190C). Grease a round 8-inch baking pan with kosher margarine.

Sift together rice, baking powder, salt and cinnamon into a medium bowl. Add sugar, margarine, golden raisins, currants and banana. Mix well. Add gelatin mixture. Beat until smooth.

Pour batter into greased pan. Bake 40 to 50 minutes. Let cool in pan several minutes. Remove from pan. Place on wire rack to cool. Makes 1 cake.

Carrot Cake

4 eggs
¾ cup plus 2 tablespoons sugar
1 grated lemon peel
2 cups ground almonds

1⅓ cups finely grated raw
carrots
1 rounded tablespoon rice flour
1 teaspoon wheat-free baking
powder (see page 96)

Preheat oven to 350F (175C). Grease a 11″ × 7″ baking pan with kosher margarine.

Separate egg whites from yolks. Place yolks, sugar and lemon in a medium bowl, or blender or food processor. Beat well or process about 5 minutes at medium speed. Add almonds and carrots; stir well. Sift flour and baking powder into a small bowl. Gradually fold them into the batter. In another small bowl, beat egg whites until they are stiff; fold them into the batter.

Pour batter into greased pan. Bake 45 minutes. Let cool in pan several minutes. Remove from pan. Place on wire rack to cool. Cut into slices. Makes 24 slices.

Tip

Omit lemon if not allowed in your diet.

Spiced Cookies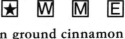

⅔ cup buckwheat flour
⅔ cup rice flour
1 tablespoon wheat-free
baking powder (see page 96)
1 teaspoon ground ginger

½ teaspoon ground cinnamon
¼ cup kosher margarine
¼ cup sugar
¼ cup light corn syrup, warmed

Preheat oven to 400F (205C). Grease a baking sheet with kosher margarine.

Sift buckwheat flour into a medium bowl twice, discarding any coarse parts. Sift together buckwheat flour, rice flour, baking powder and spices into a medium bowl twice. Cut in margarine. Add sugar and syrup; mix well.

Roll dough into balls. Place balls on greased baking sheet. Leave space between each ball for spreading. Bake 10 to 12 minutes.

Let cool on baking sheet 1 to 2 minutes. Remove cookies from sheet. Place on wire rack to cool. Makes 24 cookies.

Almond Cookies

1 cup rice flour
1½ teaspoons wheat-free
  baking powder (see page 96)
Pinch of salt
1 teaspoon pumpkin-pie spice
¼ cup olive oil

¼ cup brown sugar, packed
¼ cup sugar
1 egg, well beaten
¼ teaspoon almond extract
¼ cup sliced almonds

Preheat oven to 400F (205C). Grease a baking sheet with kosher margarine.

Sift together flour, baking powder, salt and pumpkin-pie spice into a medium bowl twice. Add oil, sugars, egg and almond extract; mix well.

Place dough on greased baking sheet 1 teaspoon at a time. Leave space between each teaspoonful for spreading. Decorate each cookie with 2 sliced almonds. Bake 10 to 12 minutes. Remove cookies from sheet. Place on wire rack to cool. Makes 18 to 20 cookies.

Coconut Cookies

1¼ cups millet flour
1 teaspoon wheat-free baking
  powder (see page 96)
⅓ cup sugar

½ cup shredded coconut
½ cup plus 2 tablespoons
  kosher margarine

Preheat oven to 325F (165C). Grease a baking sheet with kosher margarine.

Sift together flour and baking powder into a medium bowl. Add sugar and coconut; mix well. Cut in margarine; knead well.

Dust a board and rolling pin with millet flour. Roll out dough to ¼-inch thickness. Cut into rounds with a 1½-inch cookie cutter.

Place cookies on greased baking sheet. Leave space between each cookie for spreading. Bake about 15 minutes. Remove cookies from sheet. Place on wire rack to cool. Makes 20 cookies.

Orange Cookies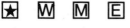

1¾ cups rice flour
1 teaspoon wheat-free baking
  powder (see page 96)
½ cup kosher margarine

1 egg, well beaten
Juice of ½ orange
Peel of ½ orange, finely grated

Preheat oven to 325F (165C). Grease a baking sheet with kosher margarine.

Sift together flour and baking powder into a medium bowl twice. Cut in margarine. Add egg, orange juice and peel; mix well.

Dust a board and rolling pin with rice flour. Roll out dough to ¼-inch thickness. Cut into rounds with a 1½-inch cookie cutter. Place cookies on greased baking sheet. Leave space between each cookie for spreading. Bake about 15 minutes. Remove cookies from sheet. Place on wire rack to cool. Makes 24 cookies.

See photograph, page 101

Ginger Cookies ★ Ⓦ Ⓜ Ⓔ

1 cup plus 2 tablespoons
  ground rice
2 tablespoons wheat-free
  baking powder (see page 96)
2 teaspoons ground ginger

¼ cup dark brown sugar, packed
⅓ cup kosher margarine
Water
Rice flour

Preheat oven to 375F (190C). Grease a baking sheet with kosher margarine.

Sift together ground rice, baking powder and ginger into a medium bowl. Add sugar. Cut in margarine until mixture has a crumbly consistency. When ingredients are well-mixed, add just enough water to obtain a soft dough.

Dust a board and rolling pin with rice flour. Roll out dough to ½-inch thickness. Cut into interesting shapes with cookie cutters. Place cookies on greased baking sheet. Leave space between each cookie for spreading. Bake 20 to 25 minutes. Remove cookies from sheet. Place on wire rack to cool. Makes 18 to 20 cookies.

Coconut Rice Cookies

⅓ cup kosher margarine, room
  temperature
¼ cup dark brown sugar, packed
1 small egg

1 cup plus 2 tablespoons
  ground rice
1 teaspoon wheat-free baking
  powder (see page 96)
¾ cup shredded coconut

Preheat oven to 375F (190C). Grease a baking sheet with kosher margarine.

Cream together margarine and sugar in a medium bowl until light and fluffy. Beat in egg. Sift the rice and baking powder into a separate medium bowl. Add coconut; mix well. Add these ingredients to creamed mixture. Beat until combined. Dust a board with rice flour. Turn out dough and knead until smooth. Roll out dough to ½-inch thickness. Cut with a ½-inch cookie cutter. Place cookies on greased baking sheet. Leave space between each cookie for spreading. Bake 15 to 20 minutes. Remove cookies from sheet. Place on wire rack to cool. Makes 18 to 20 cookies.

Carob Fingers

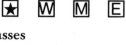

⅓ cup carob flour
Scant ½ cup ground rice
¼ cup sugar
1 teaspoon wheat-free baking
powder (see page 96)

3 tablespoons kosher margarine
½ (¼-oz.) envelope unflavored
gelatin, dissolved in ½ cup
hot water and cooled to
room temperature

Preheat oven to 350F (175C). Grease a baking sheet with kosher margarine.

Sift together flour, rice, sugar and baking powder into a large bowl. Cut in margarine. Stir in gelatin solution; mix until dough is firm. Dust a board and rolling pin with carob flour. Roll out dough to ½-inch thickness. Cut into 8 fingers. Place fingers on greased baking sheet, using a spatula. Bake 10 minutes. Remove fingers from sheet. Place on wire rack to cool. Makes 8 fingers.

Parkin

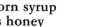

1¾ cups millet flour
1 teaspoon baking soda
2 teaspoons ground ginger
2¼ cups millet flakes
½ cup kosher margarine

⅓ cup molasses
⅓ cup light corn syrup
2 tablespoons honey
1 tablespoon brown sugar
¾ cup milk substitute

Preheat oven to 350F (175C). Grease a square 8-inch baking pan with kosher margarine.

Sift together flour, baking soda and ginger into a medium bowl. Stir in millet flakes. Place margarine, molasses, light corn syrup, honey and sugar in a medium saucepan. Heat slowly until all ingredients are melted. Remove from heat. Beat molasses mixture and milk substitute into flour mixture.

Pour into greased pan. Bake 45 to 50 minutes until firm to the touch. Let cool in pan 15 minutes. Remove from pan. Place on wire rack to cool. Cut into 2-inch squares. Makes 16 squares.

Millet-Flake Cookies

Generous ¾ cup potato flour
⅛ teaspoon salt
6 tablespoons kosher margarine,
room temperature

1 cup plus 2 tablespoons
millet flakes
2 tablespoons brown sugar
1 egg

Preheat oven to 350F (175C). Grease a baking sheet with kosher margarine.

Sift together flour and salt into a medium bowl. Add margarine; beat until well-blended. Stir in millet flakes and brown sugar. Add egg. Mix until dough is firm. Dust a board and rolling pin with potato flour. Roll out dough to ¼-inch thickness. Cut into rounds with a 2-inch cookie cutter. Prick each cookie with a fork. Place cookies on greased baking sheet. Bake 15 to 20 minutes, until cookies are golden brown. Let cool on baking sheet a few minutes. Remove from sheet. Place on wire rack to cool. Makes 25 to 30 cookies.

Date & Millet Squares ★ Ⓜ Ⓜ Ⓔ

1⅓ cups chopped dates
½ cup unsweetened apple juice
½ cup kosher margarine
¾ cup soft brown sugar, packed
¾ cup plus 1 tablespoon rice flour or millet flour
1½ cups millet flakes

Preheat oven to 350F (175C). Grease a square 8-inch baking pan with kosher margarine.

Put dates in a medium saucepan; add apple juice. Cook over low heat about 5 minutes, until mixture is soft and pulpy. Chop margarine into small pieces. Place sugar, rice flour or millet flour and millet flakes in a medium bowl. Add chopped margarine; mix until ingredients are well-blended.

Divide millet mixture in half. Press ½ of mixture firmly into bottom of baking pan. Pour date mixture over the top. Cover with remaining ½ of mixture. Press down firmly. Bake 35 to 40 minutes. Let cool in the pan. Cut into squares. Makes 16 squares.

Fruits & Puddings

Banana Cream ⬜ⓂⓋ ⬜Ⓜ ⬜Ⓔ

4 medium bananas
1 tablespoon lemon juice

1¾ cups goat's milk or sheep's
   milk yogurt
1 teaspoon honey

Place all ingredients in a blender or food processor fitted with a steel blade. Process until creamy. Cover and refrigerate until chilled. Makes 4 servings.

Italian Baked Peaches ⬜Ⓦ ⬜Ⓜ ⬜Ⓔ

6 large peaches, peeled
¾ cup ground almonds

⅓ cup soft brown sugar, packed
¼ cup unsweetened apple juice

Preheat oven to 425F (220C).
   Cut peaches in half; remove pits. Mix almonds and brown sugar in a medium bowl. Add about 1 tablespoon apple juice, just enough to bind almond mixture. Stuff peach halves with almond mixture, filling holes left by pits. Press halves together.
   Place peaches in a small baking dish. Pour remaining apple juice over peaches; cover. Bake in preheated oven until peaches are tender, about 30 minutes. Makes 6 servings.

See photograph, page 104

Poached Peaches with Raspberry Sauce ⭐ ⬜Ⓦ ⬜Ⓜ ⬜Ⓔ

⅔ cup water
½ teaspoon vanilla extract
¼ cup sugar
4 large peaches, peeled

Raspberry Sauce:
1 cup raspberries
⅓ cup powdered sugar
1½ teaspoons grape juice

In a medium saucepan, combine water, vanilla and sugar; add peaches. Poach peaches in syrup until peaches are tender, about 30 minutes. Place peaches in a medium bowl; cover and refrigerate until chilled. Prepare Raspberry Sauce. Put peaches into individual dishes. Pour sauce over peaches and serve. Makes 4 servings.

Raspberry Sauce:
Place raspberries in a small bowl. Sprinkle powdered sugar over raspberries. Spoon grape juice over mixture; marinate at least 1 hour. Place mixture in a blender or food processor fitted with a steel blade. Process until pureed. Pour through a sieve into a small bowl. Cover and refrigerate until chilled.

Apricot Puree

1 lb. fresh apricots
2½ cups water
¾ cup sugar

¼ cup unsweetened apple juice

Place apricots and water in a medium saucepan; add sugar. Bring to a boil. Reduce heat; simmer until apricots are soft. Remove apricots from pan; save syrup. Let apricots cool. Remove pits.
  Place apricots and syrup in a blender or food processor fitted with a steel blade; add apple juice. Process until pureed. Makes 4 servings.

Green Fruit Mousse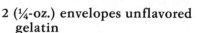

2½ cups seedless green grapes
1½ cups gooseberries, trimmed
¾ cup sugar
⅓ cup unsweetened apple juice

2 (¼-oz.) envelopes unflavored gelatin
¼ cup water
⅔ cup goat's milk yogurt
1 kiwifruit

Place the grapes, gooseberries, sugar and apple juice in a medium saucepan. Bring to a boil. Reduce heat; simmer 20 minutes. Allow to cool. Pour mixture into a blender or food processor fitted with a steel blade. Process until pureed. Pour through a sieve into a medium bowl.
  In a small saucepan, combine gelatin and water. Let stand 5 minutes. Place over low heat; stir until dissolved. Stir dissolved gelatin into puree. Stir in yogurt. Pour into 4 to 6 individual dishes. Cover and refrigerate until set.
  Just before serving, peel and slice kiwifruit. Place slices on top of mousse. Makes 4 to 6 servings.

See photograph, page 104

Glazed Pears with Golden Raisins   ★ W M E

2 ripe pears	1 tablespoon honey
¼ cup water	1 tablespoon brown sugar
2 tablespoons golden raisins	

Preheat oven to 375F (190C).
Peel pears leaving on stems. Core from base. Divide raisins between the 2 pears and use to stuff cavities. Place in a shallow baking dish; add water. Pour honey evenly over pears. Sprinkle brown sugar on top. Bake 30 minutes. Makes 2 servings.

Melon Shells with Fruit   ★ W M E A

1 melon	2½ cups red grapes, cut in half
4 peaches, sliced	and seeded

Cut melon in half lengthwise. Remove seeds. Being careful not to damage the skin, remove melon flesh; cut into cubes. Set shells aside. Put melon cubes into a medium bowl. Add peaches and grapes. Mix carefully.
Fill melon halves with fruit mixture. Chill 30 minutes. Makes 6 servings.

Variation:
Any combination of fruit fillings can be used, depending on the season. Strawberries, raspberries and nectarines work very well.

Apple Brûlée   ★ W M E

1 small baking apple, cored	¼ cup goat's milk yogurt
Granulated sugar to taste	3 tablespoons brown sugar
Water	

Stew apple in a small saucepan in as little water as possible until almost tender. Add granulated sugar. Allow to cool in water.
Preheat broiler. Place apple in a small flameproof dish. Pour yogurt on top. Sprinkle brown sugar on top. Broil until sugar melts and bubbles; watch carefully. Serve immediately. Makes 1 serving.

Fancy Fruit

1 kiwifruit, sliced crosswise 1 banana, sliced
2 peaches or nectarines, sliced 1 mango

Arrange kiwifruit slices and peach or nectarine slices alternately around edge of a plate. Place a ring of banana slices inside kiwifruit and peach slices. Using a melon baller, scoop out mango. Arrange mango balls in center of plate. Makes 2 servings.

A Taste of Summer ★ W M E

1 lb. rhubarb, chopped 1 cup sugar
½ lb. fresh black currants 1¼ cups water
1 nectarine, chopped

Mix rhubarb and fruit in a medium bowl. Put ⅓ of fruit mixture in bottom of a baking dish. Sprinkle with sugar. Add another ⅓ of fruit mixture; sprinkle with sugar. Add remaining fruit mixture; sprinkle with sugar. Cover dish with foil; fasten securely.
    Place a trivet and water in a pressure cooker. Place dish in pressure cooker on trivet. Cook at 5 pounds pressure, 7 minutes. Quickly reduce pressure by putting pressure cooker in sink and running cold water over it. Remove dish from pressure cooker. Let fruit cool to room temperature. Makes 3 servings.

Cinnamon Rhubarb

¾ lb. rhubarb, chopped 4 to 5 tablespoons granulated
¼ cup water or dark brown sugar
Pinch of ground cinnamon

Place ingredients in a medium saucepan. Cook over low heat until rhubarb is tender. Makes 3 servings.

Baked Apples ★ Ⓦ Ⓜ Ⓔ

2 large Granny Smith apples
2 tablespoons light brown sugar
2 pinches of ground cinnamon
2 pinches of freshly ground
nutmeg

2 tablespoons currants
2 whole cloves
Coconut Sauce (see page 94)

Preheat oven to 375F (190C).
Core apples, being careful not to damage peel. In a small bowl, combine sugar, cinnamon and nutmeg.
Place apples in a small baking pan. Pack centers with alternate layers of dried currants and sugar-and-spice mixture. Place 1 clove in each apple. Bake about 20 minutes or until tender. Remove cloves. Prepare Coconut Sauce. Pour over apples. Makes 2 servings.

See photograph, page 103

Black Currant & Tofu Whip ★ Ⓦ Ⓜ Ⓔ Ⓐ

1 lb. fresh black currants
Water

Sugar to taste
10 oz. tofu

Place black currants, a little water and sugar in a medium saucepan. Bring to a boil. Reduce heat; simmer until currants are soft. Let cool. Pour into blender or food processor fitted with a steel blade; add tofu. Process until pureed. Pour into a bowl. Cover and refrigerate until chilled. Makes 4 to 6 servings.

Variation:
Other fruits, such as blackberries, blueberries or gooseberries can be substituted for black currants.

See photograph, page 103

Carob Ice Cream ★ Ⓦ Ⓜ Ⓔ

¼ cup honey
2¼ cups soy milk

¼ cup sunflower oil
½ cup carob powder

Place all ingredients in a blender or food processor fitted with a steel blade. Process until blended. Pour into an ice-cream container. Freeze according to manufacturer's instructions. Makes 4 to 6 servings.

Variation:
Other flavorings, such as pureed fruit, can be substituted for carob powder.

See photograph, page 103
Millet & Hazelnut Ice Cream Ⓜ Ⓜ

¾ cup millet flakes
½ cup chopped hazelnuts
¾ cup dark brown sugar, packed

3 egg whites
1¼ cups goat's milk yogurt or
  sheep's milk yogurt

Preheat broiler. Place millet flakes, hazelnuts and ¼ cup sugar in a medium bowl. Mix well. Spread mixture on a baking sheet. Broil until browned, stirring occasionally. Let cool.

Beat egg whites in a medium bowl until soft peaks form. Gradually whisk in remaining ½ cup sugar until mixture becomes stiff and glossy. Carefully fold in yogurt and millet-and-hazelnut mixture. Pour into an ice-cream container. Freeze according to manufacturer's instructions. Makes 6 to 8 servings.

Rice & Carob Pudding Ⓜ Ⓜ Ⓔ

1¼ cups milk substitute
2 tablespoons ground rice
1 tablespoon light brown sugar
2 tablespoons shredded coconut

3 tablespoons ground almonds
2 teaspoons carob flour
Additional shredded coconut

Pour milk substitute into a medium saucepan; bring to a boil. Sprinkle rice and sugar into milk. Reduce heat. Simmer, stirring continuously, about 4 minutes, until pudding thickens. Stir in 2 tablespoons coconut, almonds and carob flour. Mix well. Sprinkle with coconut before serving. Serve warm or chilled. Makes 2 servings.

Christmas Pudding

¾ cup kosher margarine, room
temperature
1 cup brown sugar, packed
3 eggs, beaten
3½ cups mixed dried fruit
½ cup sliced almonds
1 small Golden Delicious
apple, cored, peeled and
grated

Peel of ½ orange, finely grated
½ cup potato flour
½ cup rice flour or ⅓ cup
ground rice
¼ teaspoon freshly grated
nutmeg
½ teaspoon pumpkin-pie spice
2 to 3 tablespoons brandy

Cream margarine and sugar in a medium bowl. Add eggs, a table-spoon at a time, beating continuously. Add dried fruit, almonds, apple and orange peel; mix well.

Sift together flours, nutmeg and pumpkin-pie spice into a medium bowl. Add to batter. Stir in brandy. Grease individual ovenproof bowls with margarine; fill with batter. Cover with waxed paper or foil. Place each pudding bowl on a trivet in a large pan. Add enough boiling water to come halfway up side of bowl. Steam 3 hours, adding more water if needed. Makes 1 large or 2 medium puddings.

Tip

This pudding will not keep as long as ordinary puddings. Store it in the freezer.

Custard Tart

2 eggs
2 egg whites
1¼ cups soy milk

¼ cup sugar
1 baked Sweet Pastry shell
(see page 99)

Preheat oven to 350F (175C).

Beat eggs, egg whites, soy milk and sugar in a medium bowl until well-blended. Strain mixture into pastry shell. Bake in pre-heated oven 30 to 40 minutes, until a knife inserted into center comes out clean. Serve cold. Makes 6 servings.

Autumn Tart   ★ W M E

¼ cup kosher margarine
2 pinches of ground ginger
2 cups crushed Coconut Rice
  Cookies (see page 109)
1½ lbs. mixed apples, peeled
  and chopped
½ cup water

¼ cup dark brown sugar, packed
3 whole cloves
Pinch of ground cinnamon
⅓ cup golden raisins
1 (¼-oz.) envelope unflavored
  gelatin
¼ cup water

Melt margarine in a medium saucepan. Stir in ginger, then stir in crushed cookies. Mix well. Grease a 9-inch pie plate with kosher margarine. Press cookie mixture into bottom of pie plate. Place in refrigerator to chill.

Place apples, ½ cup water, sugar, spices and golden raisins in a medium saucepan. Bring to a boil. Reduce heat; simmer, stirring gently so apple pieces do not break up. Drain apples; save cooking liquid in pan.

Add enough hot water to cooking liquid to make 1 cup. In a small saucepan, combine gelatin and ¼ cup cold water. Let stand 5 minutes. Stir gelatin mixture into hot cooking liquid until dissolved. If necessary, heat until dissolved. Remove cloves from apples. Combine apples and gelatin mixture. Refrigerate until slightly thickened. Pour into crust. Refrigerate until set. Makes 6 servings.

Variation:
Other cookies can be substituted for the Coconut Rice Cookies. If you use another cookie, omit the ginger.

ACKNOWLEDGMENTS

The authors are particularly grateful to Alison Wilson for typing the manuscript.

1986   EW
VAJ
JH

The publishers are grateful to the following for their help in preparation of this book: the photographs were taken by Ray Moller, assisted by Liz Gedney; art direction was by Valerie Wright, styling by Penny Markham and food preparation by Lisa Collard.

INDEX

Page numbers in *italic* refer to the illustrations

acid-reducing diet, 21
Addenbrooke's exclusion diet, 22–3
allergies, 8, 14
Almond Cookies, 108
Alzheimer's disease, 25
antibiotics, 9
antibodies, 8
apple: Apple & Spinach Salad, 50
  Apple & Walnut Loaf, 98
  Apple Brûlée, 114
  Autumn Tart, 119
  Baked Apples, 116
  Bean & Apple Dip, 64, *92*
  Blackberry & Apple Jelly, 95
  Curried Apple & Carrot Soup,
   41, 48
  Date & Apple Filled Pancakes,
   36
  Mackerel with Apples, 72
  Pork & Apple Pie, 76
  Pork Chops with Apples
   & Ginger, 76, *91*
  Salsify & Apple Soup, 48
  Split-Pea Cutlets with Apple
   Rings, 61
  Zucchini & Apple salad, 51
apricot: Apricot Filled Pancakes,
  36–7
  Apricot Milk Shake, 37
  Apricot Purée, 113
  Chicken with Fruit, *80*, 85
Arabian Lamb, 75
arthritis, 10, 11–12, 16, 21–4
asthma, 9, 17
Autumn Tart, 119
Avocado Dip, 40

bacteria, 9
Baked Apples, 116
Baked Stuffed Trout, 68, *69*
Baked Zucchini, 54
baking powder, 96
banana: Banana Bread, 97
  Banana Cake, 106
  Banana Cream, 112
  Eggless Banana Cake, 106

  Oriental Banana Salad, 52
  Simple Banana Loaf, 97
Bean & Apple Dip, 64, *92*
Bean & Pepper Salad, 50
Bean Salad, 49
beansprouts: Oriental Chicken, 85
  Oriental Vegetables, 65–6
beef: Beef & Lentils, 74–5
  Beef with Vegetables, 74, *82*
  Bobotie, 78–83, *79*
  Dolmades, *44*, 45
  Yorkshire Potted Beef, 74
Beef & Carrot Salad, 51
beverages, 38–9
Black Currants: Black currant &
  Tofu Whip, *103*, 116
  Black Currant Jam, 94
  A Taste of Summer, 115
Blackberry & Apple Jelly, 95
blood analysis, 15
Bobotie, 78–83, *79*
bread, 96–9
Breakfast Fruit Soup, 37
breakfasts, 36–7
buckwheat, 31
  Buckwheat Pancakes, 36
  Eggplant & Buckwheat pasta, *43*,
   58

caffeine, 8
cakes, 100–7
canned foods, 25
carob, 30
  Carob Fingers, 110
  Carob Ice Cream, *103*, 116
  Rice & Carob Pudding, 117
carrot: Beet & Carrot Salad, 51
  Carrot Cake, 107
  Curried Apple & Carrot Soup,
   41, 48
cauliflower: Marinated Pea &
  Cauliflower Salad, 52
Celery Soup, 47
cheese: Cheese Dip, 63
  Cheese Fruit & Nut Loaf, 66, *70*
  Eggplant Supper, 57

Salad Dip, 64
chicken: Chicken & Rice, 87
   Chicken in a Coconut, 86
   Chicken in Mango Sauce, 87–8
   Chicken with Fruit, *80*, 85
   Crispy Chicken with Herbed
      Tomatoes, 88
   Curried Chicken Salad, 51
   Oriental Chicken, 85
   Spicy Chicken, 86
   Spicy Chicken Salad, 87
   stuffing for, 84
Chicken Liver Salad, 46
children, hyperactivity, 10, 12–13
Chinese-Style Tofu, 56
Christmas Pudding, 118
Cinnamon Rhubarb, 115
coconut: Chicken in a Coconut, 86
   Coconut & Raspberry Jelly
      Roll, 100–5, *101*
   Coconut Cookies, 108
   Coconut Loaf, 96
   Coconut Rice Cookies, 109
   Coconut Sauce, 94
cod: Fish Curry, 72
Colorful Lentils, 61–2
Cookies, 107–11
cooking utensils, 25–6
corn, 28
Corsican Liver, 84
cow's milk sensitive enteropathy,
   10
Cream of Artichoke Soup, 49
Crispy Chicken with Herbed
   Tomatoes, 88
Crohn's disease, 10–11, 17
Crudités, 40
cucumber: Cucumber Dip, 63, *92*
   Trout with Cucumber, 68
curry: Bobotie, 78–83, *79*
   Curried Apple & Carrot Soup,
      41, 48
   Curried Chicken Salad, 51
   Curried Parsnip Soup, 47
   Fish Curry, 72
   Lima-Bean Curry, 57
   Vegetable Curry, 60
Custard Tart, 118
cytotoxic test, 14–15

dates: Date & Apple Filled
   Pancakes, 36
Date & Millet Squares, 111

Date & Walnut Loaf, 98, *102*
Deep-Fried Mung Beans, 64, *92*
Deviled Kidneys, 83
diarrhea, 9, 14
dips: Avocado, 40
   Bean & Apple, 64,*92*
   Cheese, 63
   Cucumber, 63, *92*
   Salad, 64
Dolmades, *44*, 45
Dong, Dr., 21
drinks, 38–9
duck: Duck with Olives, 89
   Marinated Duck, 89

eczema, 8, 10, 17
Egg-Free Mayonnaise, 93
Eggless Banana Cake, 106
Eggless Fruit Cake, 100
eggplant: Eggplant & Buckwheat
      Pasta, *43*, 58
   Eggplant Purée, 40–5, *41*
   Eggplant Supper, 57
Eggs, 29
   substitutes for, 30
enzyme deficiencies, 8
Eskimos, 21
exclusion diets, 17–20, 22–4

Fancy Fruit, 115
Feingold, Dr. Ben, 12
fish, 70–3
   Baked Stuffed Trout, 68, *69*
   Fish Cakes, *69*, 73
   Fish Curry, 72
   Fish with Sorrel Sauce, 71
   Trout with Cucumber, 68
food labeling, 25
fruit, 112–16
   Breakfast Fruit Soup, 37
   Mixed Fruit Cocktail, 39
fruit, dried: Cheese Fruit & Nut
      Loaf, 66, *70*
   Christmas Pudding, 118
   Eggless Fruit Cake, 100
   Fruit & Nut Snack, 67, *70*
   Mixed Dried Fruit, 37

Garam Masala, 30
garbanzo beans: Garbanzo-Bean
      Pancake, 67, *70*
   Garbanzo Beans and Tomatoes,
      66
ginger: Ginger Cookies, *101*, 109

Gingerroot Tea, 38
Pork Chops with Apples &
Ginger, 76, *91*
Glazed Pears with Golden Raisins,
104, 114
gluten, 10
gluten-free products, 30
gluten sensitive enteropathy, 9
Golden Raisins, Glazed Pears with,
104, 114
gout, 11, 21
Granola, 35
grape leaves: Dolmades, *44*, 45
Green & White Salad, *42*, 52
Green Bell Pepper Sauce, 93
Green Fruit Mousse, 113

hair tests, 15
Halibut, Italian, 71
Hazelnut & Millet Ice Cream, *103*,
117
Honey Cake, *101*, 105–6
hyperactivity, 10, 12–13, 14, 17

ice cream, *103*, 116–17
Indian Millet with Yellow Split
Peas, 60–1
irritable bowel syndrome, 7, 9, 17
Italian Baked Peaches, 112
Italian Halibut, 71

jam: Black-Currant Jam, 94
Blackberry & Apple Jelly, 95
Plum Jam, 95
Raspberry or Loganberry Jam,
94
Jelly Roll, Coconut & Raspberry,
100–5, *101*

Kidneys, Deviled, 83
kiwifruit: Tomato & Kiwifruit
Salad, 52

lamb: Arabian Lamb, 75
Bobotie, 78–83, *79*
Oriental Stuffed Lamb, 78, *79*
Stuffed Lamb Shoulder, 75
lentils: Beef & Lentils, 74–5
Colorful Lentils, 61–2
Lentil Rissoles, 62
Lima-Bean Curry, 57
liver: Chicken Liver Salad, 46
Corsican Liver, 84

Turkey Liver Pâté, 46
Loganberry Jam, 94

Mackerel with Apples, 72
mango: Chicken in Mango Sauce,
87–8
margarine, 31
Marinated Duck, 89
Marinated Fried Tofu, *42*, 56
Marinated Pea & Cauliflower
Salad, 52
Marinated Pork, 77
Mary's Salmon Delight, *44*, 45–6
Mayonnaise, Egg-Free, 93
meat, 74–84
Melon Shells with Fruit, 114
migraine, 7, 9, 10, 14, 17
milk, 8, 10, 14, 29
Milk Shake, Apricot, 37
millet, 31
Date & Millet Squares, 111
Granola, 35
Indian Millet with Yellow Split
Peas, 60–1
Millet & Hazelnut Ice Cream,
103, 117
Millet-Flake Cookies, 110–11
Muesli, 35
Raspberry & Millet Crunch, 35–6
minerals, 15
mint: Tea with Fresh Mint, 38
miso, 31
Mixed Dried Fruit, 37
Mixed Fruit Cocktail, 39
Mousse, Green Fruit, 113
Muesli, 35
Mung Beans, Deep-Fried, 64, *92*
mushrooms: Mushrooms with
Cilantro, *42–3*, 55
Oriental Vegetables, 65–6

nuts: Cheese Fruit & Nut Loaf, 66,
70
Fruit & Nut Snack, 67, *70*
okra: Oriental Vegetables, 65–6
Olives, Duck with, 89
Orange Cookies, 108–9
Oriental Banana Salad, 52
Oriental Chicken, 85
Oriental Stuffed Lamb, 78, *79*
Oriental Vegetables, 65–6
osteoarthritis, 11

Pâté, Turkey Liver, 46
Paella, Vegetarian, 59
pancakes: Apricot Filled Pancakes, 36-7
Buckwheat Pancakes, 36
Date & Apple Filled Pancakes, 36
Garbanzo-Bean Pancake, 67, *70*
Savory Pancake Filling, 65, *70*
Parkin, 110
parsnip: Curried Parsnip Soup, 47
Pasta, Buckwheat, with Eggplant, *43*, 58
pastry, 99
peach: Italian Baked Peaches, 112
Poached Peaches with Raspberry Sauce, *104*, 112-13
Peanut Milk, 38
Pears, Glazed, with Golden Raisins, *104*, 114
peas: Marinated Pea & Cauliflower Salad, 52
peas, split: Indian Millet with Yellow Split Peas, 60-1
Split-Pea Cutlets with Apple Rings, 61
Vegetable Curry, 60
peppers, bell: Bean & Pepper Salad, 50
Chicken in a Coconut, 86
Colorful Lentils, 61-2
Green Bell Pepper Sauce, 93
Pork & Bell Pepper Casserole, 77
Stuffed Peppers, 58-9
Plum Jam, 95
Poached Peaches with Raspberry Sauce, *104*, 112-13
pork: Marinated Pork, 77
Pork & Apple Pie, 76
Pork & Bell Pepper Casserole, 77
Pork Chops with Apples & Ginger, 76, *91*
potato: Pork & Apple Pie, 76
poultry, 84-9
preservatives, 7
Pressed Tongue, 77-8
Prune-Striped Turkey, *80*, 88-9
puddings, 112-19
purées, 90

radioallergosorbent test (RAST), 8, 14
Raita, Walnut, 93
raspberry: Poached Peaches with Raspberry Sauce, *104*, 112-13
Raspberry & Millet Crunch, 35-6
Raspberry Jam, 94
Red Cabbage, 54
red kidney beans: Bean & Apple Dip, 64, *92*
Beef with Vegetables, 74, *82*
rheumatoid arthritis, 12, 21-4
rhinitis, 9, 17
rhubarb: Cinnamon Rhubarb, 115
A Taste of Summer, 115
rice, 31
Chicken & Rice, 87
Rice Tabbouleh, 59
Rice Tea, 38
Stuffed Peppers, 58-9
Turmeric Rice, 58
Vegetarian Paella, 59
rice, ground, 30
Coconut Rice Cookies, 109
Rice & Carob Pudding, 117
Rice Sponge Cake, 105
Rissoles, Lentil, 62

Salad Dip, 64
salads, 49-52
Apple & Spinach Salad, 50
Bean & Pepper Salad, 50
Bean Salad, 49
Carrot & Beet Salad, 51
Chicken Liver Salad, 46
Curried Chicken Salad, 51
Green & White Salad, 52
Marinated Pea & Cauliflower Salad, 52
Oriental Banana Salad, 53
Spicy Chicken Salad, 87
Tomato & Kiwifruit Salad, 52
Zucchini & Apple Salad, 51
salmon: Mary's Salmon Delight, *44*, 45-6
Salsify & Apple Soup, 48
saucepans, 25-6
sauces, 93-4
Savory Pancake Filling, 65, *70*
Scones, Yogurt & Raisin, 99, *102*
Simple Banana Loaf, 97

skin tests, 14
snacks, 63–7
sorrel: Fish with Sorrel Sauce, 71
soups, 47–9
  Breakfast Fruit Soup, 37
  Celery Soup, 47
  Cream of Artichoke Soup, 49
  Curried Apple & Carrot Soup, 48
  Curried Parsnip Soup, 47
  Salsify & Apple Soup, 48
  Spinach & Tomato Soup, 47–8
soy products, 31
soy milk, 31
Spiced Cookies, 107
Spicy Chicken, 86
Spicy Chicken Salad, 87
spinach: Apple & Spinach Salad, 50
  Spinach & Tomato Soup, 47–8
Split-Pea Cutlets with Apple Rings, 61
Stir-Fried Mixed Vegetables, 55
stocks, 90
Stuffed Lamb Shoulder, 75
Stuffed Peppers, 58–9
Stuffing for Roast Chicken, 84
Sweet Pastry, 99
Sweet Yogurt Drink, 39

tamari, 31
tartrazine, 8
tarts: Autumn Tart, 119
  Custard Tart, 118
A Taste of Summer, 115
tea, 38–9
tests, 14–16
tofu, 31
  Black Currant & Tofu Whip, *103*, 116
  Chinese-Style Tofu, 56
  Marinated Fried Tofu, *42*, 56

Tofu Spread, 63, *92*
tomato: Baked Zucchini, 54
  Crispy Chicken with Herbed Tomatoes, 88
  Garbanzo Beans & Tomatoes, 66
  Italian Halibut, 71
  Spinach & Tomato Soup, 47–8
  Tomato & Kiwifruit Salad, 52
  Tomato Cocktail, 39
Tongue, Pressed, 77–8
tongue test, 14
trout: Baked Stuffed Trout, 68, *69*
  Trout with Cucumber, 68
Turkey, Prune-Striped, *80*, 88–9
Turkey Liver Pâté, 46
Turmeric Rice, 58

urticaria, 8, 10

veal: Dolmades, *44*, 45
vegetables, 54–5
  Crudités, 40
  Vegetable Curry, 60
Vegetarian Dishes, 56–62
Vegetarian Paella, 59

walnuts: Apple & Walnut Loaf, 98
  Date & Walnut Loaf, 98, *102*
  Walnut Raita, 93
wheat, 27

yeast, 28
yogurt: Banana Cream, 112
  Cheese Dip, 63
  Cucumber Dip, 63, *92*
  Sweet Yogurt Drink, 39
  Walnut Raita, 93
  Yogurt & Raisin Scones, 99, *102*
Yorkshire Potted Beef, 74

zucchini: Baked Zucchini, 54
  Zucchini & Apple Salad, 51